Wednesdays with Winston

A Collection of Essays and Poems

by

The Grant Street Writers

Wednesdays with Winston: A Collection of Essays and Poems by The Grant Street Writers

First Edition

ISBN: 978-0-9997195-0-3 (print)
ISBN: 978-0-9997195-1-0 (ebook)

Published by The Grant Street Writers
Cover design by The Grant Street Writers and Susannah Davidson
Interior design by Kat Wertzler
Printed in the United States of America

Dedicated to Women's Voices Everywhere

Table of Contents

[1] Previously appeared in *Monsters, Myths and Other Matters* by The Budlong Woods Writers

[2] Previously appeared in *Seasons of Our Lives, Volume 2*

[3] Previously appeared on MEaction.net

[4] Previously appeared in *Tales of Our Lives, Forks in the Road, Volume 2*

Introduction

Several years ago, for reasons as diverse as our ages and backgrounds, we all signed up for a personal essay writing class. In time, and after many shared classes, we decided to meet independently, and *Wednesdays with Winston* was born. And so, every Wednesday afternoon, we gathered and were joined by Winston, a cute little rescue dog, who was omnipresent, hoping for someone to sneak him a treat. We came to learn, to write, to share . . . to laugh, to cry, and ultimately to bond in ways that we hadn't counted on.

Week after week, with Winston as constant companion, we wrote our stories replete with the joys and sadness of living our lives as daughters, sisters, wives, mothers, grandmothers and friends. We became better writers, better story tellers, better women in the process. Somewhere along the way, we became something else. We became friends. The kind of friends that only women can be to one another. Friends who can finish one another's sentences, know without asking when something is very right or very wrong, and provide support without question or hesitation. Friends who can even make sense out of an hour spent talking over one another.

This book is the result of a wealth of Wednesdays with Winston. It has been a labor of love and contains some of the best work of The Grant Street Writers. If you enjoy reading it even half as much as we enjoyed writing it, our goals will be realized.

Remembering

Snow Day

Marie Davidson

The day I almost died was one of sublime winter beauty. The sun did not warm but illuminated the world with a blazing light, in a perfect blue sky, air so fresh and cold that my nostrils vibrated with every in-breath. This kind of day only happened after a major storm. My neighborhood became a community united in the effort of digging out. I woke to the beat of metal shovels scraping against pavement. In 1957 there were no snow blowers.

It was a glorious day off for the children of the neighborhood. I had listened hopefully to the radio the night before and shouted, "Snow day! Snow day!" when I heard the mayor announce, "All public schools in Boston will be closed tomorrow due to the snowstorm." An added bonus was that my afternoon Catechism class at the local Catholic school would be cancelled, too. What a blessing. I would not only be flying free down the hill with all my sledding friends, but I would be spared the droning voice of Sister Mary Benjamin and her sourpuss warnings about how important it was to die in a state of grace. Just last week she had said we had to keep our souls "clean and tidy, because you never know the exact hour or moment of your death." Sister reminded us our best chance to get to heaven was to pray a perfect Act of Contrition just before we died.

As a ten-year-old I was lucky to have the George Wright Municipal Golf Course in my backyard. It was like having a well-cared-for playground just beyond the chain link fence. In summer, the area we called The Nursery was our baseball field. It was tucked away from the main golfing action, where my friends and I didn't get chased off by Officer Hackett, the motorcycle security cop. Next to The Nursery was The Swamp, a marshy area of scrubby vegetation and drooping trees, with a rich smell of rotting plants and an active population of insects and brave amphibians who didn't run away from us. It was the perfect place for games of Pirate Explorers and Witch in the Cellar. In the humid afternoons we would walk to the Clubhouse and buy chips and Cokes. We were tolerated as paying customers and felt very grownup among the golfers.

But the best feature of my personal golf course playground was the sledding hill. Every weekend in winter when there was enough snow on the ground, the neighborhood children would push their sleds under a section of the fence two generations of children had pulled up from the bottom and then dug a shallow trench underneath. We would follow our sleds under and pull them up to the top of the hill on the other side of the Fairway, just past the tee for the second hole. The hill was exactly the right height and angle of descent for a thrilling ride. It also came with some risk, although our parents had no idea. They thought we were perfectly safe—no automobiles to worry about, no pond to fall into, and no golf course law enforcement to chase us away.

Nature protects nothing but itself, however, and my magnificent sledding hill had a rugged side, dotted with trees and filled with bumps. It belonged to the Rough, where the slices and hooks of less skilled golfers sent many balls that were never found. After a winter storm, the defects in the Rough were covered with snow. The children of the neighborhood knew to sled on the safe Fairway side of the hill, the part that was groomed for the golfers.

The day of my brush with death, I had a shiny aluminum "flying saucer" for my sledding equipment. It was inspired by the space race with the Russians, who had launched the satellite Sputnik in October. My saucer had looked very fine under the Christmas tree, with a big red bow tied to one of the rope handgrips. I understood that, as a nation, we had to do everything possible to beat the Russians in space, and my flying saucer was a part of that effort. I left my Flexible Flyer, with its handles that guided the sled, propped up against my basement wall.

I was invincible.

As I trudged across the Fairway, pulling my saucer, I thought about Sister Mary Benjamin's teachings about sin. It was so complicated. There were venial sins. They were kind of like misdemeanors. There were mortal sins. They were kind of like felonies. And there was something called "near occasions of sin," which sounded like life in general. You had to be full up to the brim with grace to go right to heaven when you died. I thought about the condition of my soul—not very tidy. I had watched my girlfriend Eileen shoplift a lipstick at Woolworth's and said nothing. And there were those daily mean thoughts I had about my annoying older brother.

My first few runs down the sledding hill were exhilarating. The saucer rotated as it flew down, almost like an amusement ride. The sledding conditions improved all morning as our sleds tamped the top snow down and made our paths smoother and faster. All around me I heard the whoops of my friends and the whoosh of their sleds. When the sun had moved close to the top of the sky I was feeling the pull to go home for lunch and to dry out my wet boots and clothes. Just before my last run, I was thinking about tuna salad on toast and a mug of cocoa.

In hindsight, I started off too close to the edge of the hill. I couldn't steer the saucer like my Flexible Flyer, so when it veered to the right onto the Rough I knew I was going to have to make the best of it. I hit a big bump. The saucer flew straight up and plopped back down as I held on with all my might. I came back to earth facing backward. Now I was hurtling down the hill blind. I looked over my shoulder and saw I was headed at a large tree. It was coming up fast. I tried shifting my weight side to side to move away but the saucer had its own agenda.

No time for a perfect Act of Contrition. Death was seconds away. Instinct took over. I let go of the rope handles and self-ejected from my saucer, landing in a soft pile of snow that cocooned me and stopped my forward flight. My flying saucer flew on, slammed into the tree, and folded in half with a loud crack of bending metal.

I lay on my back, staring up at the brilliant blue sky, listening to my heartbeat.

I was alive. And I was really hungry.

My Grandma Rose Is a Rose

Trudi Goodman

The ride to Fox River Heights took us about two hours, and I drove my parents crazy the entire time. *Are we there yet? Ma, come on, how much longer?* Between the annoying questions and my sister and I taking turns throwing up from riding in the rumble seat of our 1939 Ford, I'm grateful Ma and Dad never left us somewhere along that road we traveled between Chicago and St. Charles, Illinois.

At the end of our journey, the bets were on as to how many mice would be found dead in the corners of Grandma's two-bedroom cottage, where rat poison was strategically placed around the rooms at the end of every summer. The cottage always released a musty smell when first opened, serving to remind us of the damp winter air and snow that crept through the places not totally sealed up when we vacated on Labor Day. Eventually the sweet prairie breeze would take over and settle in for July and August, the two months we occupied the cottage each year. The kerosene lamps were uncovered, the outhouse got a new coat of whitewash, the water pump was oiled, and the first bucket of water was brought into the house. We are back, dear cottage, we are back.

For the summers of my childhood, my parents would leave me alone with my Grandma Rose and show up only on the weekends. I adored my Grandma, and she returned that love by allowing me to roam the countryside, barefoot and fancy-free, free to explore and dream without pause.

She was the law, and her routine was simple to follow. In the morning for breakfast, toast with butter, sugar, and cinnamon, oatmeal or sometimes Cream of Wheat, and a half-cup of coffee mixed with a half-cup of milk. Have lunch when you're hungry, dinner at sundown. I took baths in steel tubs that were stationed all summer long on the lawn and filled with sun-warmed rainwater. Sometimes, when there was a shortage of rain, she and I would walk down to the Fox River, half asleep at 6 a.m., carrying with us our Ivory soap—it floats! Grandma Rose would always say, *The early bird catches the worm.*

At that time of day the beach was always deserted. There was no interruption to the quiet of the morning, only our voices, the call of an occasional songbird and the hoot of an owl. Together we would submerge into the icy cold, gray water, pull our swimsuits away from our bosoms, cup our hands and gently splash water onto our bodies, gradually adjusting to the chill of the river. Each time I splashed the cold water on me I would gasp and she would respond, *You can do it, Toots!* Her favorite name for me was Toots, and she firmly believed I could do anything.

Those summers with Grandma set me free from the scheduled life I lived as a city school child for the other ten months of the year. I enjoyed many differences in my times spent with Grandma Rose, but the biggest was my unusual bedtime. It was unusual because, unlike most other eight-year-old kids, I was allowed a night life the likes of which I would never see again.

My Grandma Rose, who spent all her childhood on a farm in Indiana as a regular farm girl, got married, gave birth to eight healthy babies, cooked and cleaned just like all the other women of her generation. Despite her conventional beginnings, this very ordinary woman ultimately became a HOTSHOT POKER-PLAYING GRANDMA in Fox River Heights. Every evening, from about 8 p.m. to midnight, she could be found along with all the other grandmas, in the back room of Ruthie's grocery and candy store, sweating over a penny ante poker game. While most other children were getting ready for bed, I got to go with her to Ruthie's. The only rule was that this time was hers, and I was never allowed to interrupt it. I would sit in a corner of the room observing her serious poker face while she shuffled and dealt the cards. The wrinkles and sculptured blue veins of her arthritic but very capable strong hands revealed that she was a woman who had traveled a long distance in her life. Her vitality and energy said that she had a long way to go . . . a lot more poker hands to play, a lot more to say.

I was entertained watching her and her plump gray-haired lady cohorts cussing and beating their fists on a well-worn oak table covered in oilcloth. They dressed in cotton swirls and shawls. Their chubby legs were encased in silk stockings secured with rubber bands rolled below the knees, and their feet were supported by heavy, black laced-up oxfords. Their aging faces were scrubbed clean and left pink and shiny. I remember Grandma Rose wearing lipstick only on special occasions. Her favorite color, Chinese Red, was purchased from a Woolworth Five and Dime. The vision of Grandma Rose and her poker-playing buddies sitting around the table with only a Tiffany light hanging above them recalled a scene from a Norman Rockwell painting.

After several hours of *Oh Hells* and *Damn Its*, accompanied by the constant clink, clink of tossed copper pennies, I often got tired, bored and cranky. I would beg to go home, and she would say, *One more hand,*

Toots, it's only 11:30. Go count the dead flies on the Flypaper. That'll give you something to do. I'm throwing in the towel soon. Nothing but rotten cards the whole evening.

With an undefeated smile on her face, she would slam the screen door behind her, dramatically announcing her departure, as though she were on stage elegantly exiting stage right. Always the lady, she'd say, *Goodnight, girls, I'm going home. Let's go, Toots!* And we were out the door. While she never told me, from outward appearances I knew that I was her favorite grandchild. I kept it my secret.

There were no streetlights in the country, and the nights were ink black. We walked home following the road by the light of the moon and stars and the beam of one small flashlight. If ever I said I was afraid, Grandma Rose would laugh and say, *What's to be afraid of?* She protected me as we made our way back to the small white cabin. Because small animals roamed the prairie and the surrounding forest in the middle of the night, using the outdoor plumbing at 2 a.m. was not a good idea. And so, before lights out, Grandma Rose would place flower-decorated chamber potty bowls in our shared bedroom. I tried, but never got the hang of those bowls.

No matter what time she went to bed, Grandma Rose was up at the crack of dawn, and like a morning bugle call, she would blare out another of her sayings . . . *Rise and shine, Folks!* I was the Folks.

The year Grandma Rose announced that she was following several of her children to California, I was thirteen years old, and I thought my life was over. All my tears did not change her mind. All the tears in the world would not have changed her decision. She sold her cottage and left me. The thought that I would never see her again, because that is exactly what I thought, became too difficult, so we never said goodbye to one another.

And, for quite awhile, I lost my heart.

Life changed drastically soon after Grandma Rose left Chicago. My father's business failed, and he made his family promise not to tell anyone that he took a job driving a cab at night. That same year, when I started high school I got a part-time after-school job to help out. Ma also went to work. Grandma Rose did not know about our problems. Those were the days when the cost of long-distance communication allowed for untold stories and white lies. Probably keeping our secret from her was a good thing. I wanted her to be happy, grow old without worries, without harsh winters, and enjoy lots of poker games.

The miles between us became the barrier. I saw her only three or four times very briefly over the years before she died. Although my memories of her stop at the age of thirteen, they are my happiest memories.

New Shoes

Ruth Sterlin

As a child, my understanding of love was mostly about things. When I became attached to a pair of shoes, for example, usually ones with quiet rubber soles that would help me to steal away without being heard, I would hang onto them for dear life. They were like buddies, another arm or leg. I wouldn't let my mother clean, polish or do anything to them, except maybe change their shoelaces when there was no more room to tie another knot if one of them broke.

My mother's passion was for dresses. She often told stories of her girlhood with six siblings and how she yearned for a new dress. Coming from a poor immigrant family, there was never enough money, and all of her dresses were hand-me-downs. She described her two lonely dresses, hanging in her section of the closet. It's no wonder that by the time I was nine, my mother's closet was bursting. It reached a point that my Aunt Bruna – my mother's *bossy* older sister – would tell her to *stop buying clothes for herself now that she had three children.*

Undoubtedly, my mother was disappointed that I turned out to be a tomboy. I could outrun most of the boys who lived in our courtyard and spent my free time catching snakes and frogs with them in the swamp by my school.

"Will you *ever* wash up and comb your hair without being asked forty times?" my mother would grumble with a sigh.

Being a tomboy also limited my clothing interests to shoes that I had carefully broken in and that I knew would carry me to victory across the grassy mall behind our apartment during summertime races with my friends. My first pair of patent leather mary jane shoes – just for dress – changed things, though. They were the first clue that I was broadening my tastes. My mary janes were black and so shiny that when I gazed at them in their box, I could see my face reflected in the toe of each shoe. For them, I would put on a party dress without complaining.

My love of shoes continued to grow, and before long, my excitement would build whenever my mother announced that my everyday shoes *were on their last legs.* That meant new shoes!

On one occasion, I nagged my mother about it, asking her over and over when we were going to the shoe store. "*Thursday* we're going to buy you shoes," she reminded me with annoyance in her voice. When Thursday finally came, I didn't take in a whit of fourth-grade math waiting for the final bell to ring. As soon as I got home, my mother made me wash my face and comb my hair before we walked over to the shoe store in the plaza near our house.

The store smelled of new shoes and leather. I looked around while my mother was checking something inside of her purse. In all things not pertaining to her closet, she was very careful about how much money we spent. For example, even though we were a family of five, she would never cook more than one pound of spaghetti for dinner, which she served covered in spaghetti sauce. After his plateful, my older brother, *who was growing like a weed,* would fill up the rest of his stomach with peanut butter and jelly sandwiches or soup, leaving the empty can under his bed.

After my mother spoke to the floor salesman, he went behind a curtain and emerged with four shoeboxes, two under each arm. He piled the boxes on the floor and my mother went through them, asking the price of each pair. Based on her accounting, she narrowed the range to two pairs: blue leather mary janes – which I reached for immediately – and brown and white leather oxfords with white tops and tongues surrounded by dark brown leather. I tried on both pairs, testing for size by inserting my feet into the x-ray machines that were popular in shoes stores in the fifties. Each time, I could see the bones of my feet inside the shoe's outline. My mother looked too. Were the shoes wide enough? Did they pinch? Was there room to grow?

It didn't take long for me to see that my mother had already cast her vote. When I picked up the mary janes a second time, my mother matter-of-factly took them from my hands.

"Those won't last a minute, the way you run around," she said.

Then, handing me the oxfords, my mother smiled at me. She didn't smile often, and wanting to prolong the moment, I smiled back, keeping my disappointment to myself.

"Okay, Mom, the brown ones!" I said mustering up a cheery tone.

By this time, though, she was already halfway to the cash register with her wallet out. As she passed the salesman several dollar bills, I glanced longingly back at the blue mary janes, one shoe sitting in its box and the other rolled over on its side on the floor.

That night, I showed my new oxfords to my dad. He took a quick look and from behind his newspaper, I heard "Hm-m-m nice shoes!" I tried to be happy about them. It would have helped if he had sounded more enthusiastic, but his eyes remained glued to his newspaper.

At bedtime, I inhaled the smell of my new shoes several times. Maybe they wouldn't be so bad. Finally, I fell asleep.

The next morning, I put on my new shoes first thing, even before I took off my pajamas. Looking at them, I sat back down on my bed, my eyelids heavy with sleep. I felt deflated and had little appetite for breakfast.

On the way to school the heels of my new oxfords made tiny *clump* sounds against the sidewalk. I stopped three times to look at the bottom of my shoes. They felt stiff and uncomfortable. *I hate oxfords,* I said to myself. During recess, some of the boys were looking at my shoes and laughing. I kicked the dirt by the school's brick wall, not feeling like playing with my friends. No one else in the whole school, the whole world, had on oxford tie shoes. I thought about the blue mary janes in the store and tried to remember my mother's smile.

Oy to the World

Trudi Goodman

When I was a young girl in school I wanted to be Catholic. If I were a Catholic, life would be easier, happier, and so much more fun. I could have Christmas. I would belong. No longer would I be on the outside looking in. From my perspective the entire world, except for my family, celebrated Christmas. The opposing side was represented by my parents. "But you're Jewish and Jewish people don't celebrate that holiday." They would explain the reasons again and again. Nothing they said made it any easier to accept my fate. I was the only Jewish girl in the third grade at Ryerson Elementary School in Chicago. Actually, the only Jewish girl in the entire school except for the one in the first grade who happened to be my sister. I never really counted her as one of the kids in my school. At home we shared a bedroom and hours of sisterhood, but when I was away from home I usually tried to forget about her. So, for the sake of this story, I'll continue on with the drama of my being the only Jewish child in the neighborhood trying to fit in and wishing to be understood.

I was eight years old in 1942 when anti-Semitism was at an all-time high. The Jews were being blamed for the war in Europe along with the ever-popular belief that they killed G-D. So Mom never let me leave home without reminding me, "If anyone asks you what you are (meaning most certainly they want to know your religion), you say you are an American. Anything else is really none of their business."

I had experienced some memorable bullying from the kids in my neighborhood, ranging from verbal abuse—with phrases like, "You dirty Jew, you killed Christ."—to physical attacks that left me with a few scars. My only defense at that time was, "I don't know anyone with that name. Who is Christ?"

My friends said that they believed that the Jews killed Christ, but somehow I should be entitled to receive gifts in honor of his birth because he forgives his trespassers. When he was born, there must have been plenty of gifts around partly because of the Wise Men who travelled a great distance bearing gifts to honor him. So I imagined that the purpose of Santa Claus coming down from the North Pole was to reenact the beautiful journey that the Wise Men took. Now you might be wondering how this Jewish girl knew so much about Christianity. The simple answer is I learned it in school . . . public school. This was, of course, many years before public school educators decided Chanukah should get equal billing.

At just about the time all of America was sitting at tables enjoying their turkey dinner, books about Christmas were being delivered to Chicago elementary schools to await the return of students from Thanksgiving break. And, by the way, the same time the books appeared, so did the colors red and green in all forms, from lights to paper to ornaments, and they were joined by lots of glitz. The colors and decorations for Christmas never failed to take on a life of their own.

And so began my campaign for my very own Christmas. A Christmas that was perfect just like that of everyone else in the world, just like that described in the books I'd read depicting beautiful blue-eyed blonde girls and boys sitting around decorated pine trees. I was determined to have my own Christmas tree, and I dreamed of how I would decorate it. I also imagined myself on Santa Claus's knee, rattling off my list of toys and games.

Christmas carols had their own set of problems that were hard for my friends to understand. I myself barely understood when my parents said, "You will not sing songs about Christ."

"But why?" I asked.

"We don't believe in him."

"Can't I just sing *Jingle Bells* and mouth the Jesus songs?"

"No, no, and no is no!"

Ma would give me the same stupid answer each time I'd ask. However, as silly as I thought this rule was, I dared not take a chance in case it was true that Jewish people would be struck dead if they ever sang the praises of Jesus. Better safe than sorry! So with a written request from my mother, I was excused from singing those gorgeous songs that I had come to love. Besides all that, I had greater battles ahead of me.

I was still conspiring. If only I could talk to Santa. He would never know I was Jewish.

"Mom, Dad, just this once, please, please, please can I have a tree and a visit with Santa Claus? I promise I'll never mention Jesus, say the rosary or cross my heart and hope to die."

My worn-out parents finally grew tired of hearing me beg and they buckled. My persistence paid off, and my rewards were a pine tree and a trip to Santa Claus.

When the day arrived to visit Santa, he was stationed at Chicago's Marshall Field's department store. The wait was nerve-wracking because I was in dire fear of being discovered. I imagined the guard coming over and announcing to the world. "EVERYONE, your attention please, we have a Jew amongst us trying to visit Santa Claus!" And that surely would be the end of my dream come true. I was also worried that Santa would ask, "Little girl, where have you been all these years?"

Finally, it was my turn. I smiled brightly to reassure him that I came from a good and caring family, and climbed on his knee.

"So, curly top, what do you want for Christmas? Have you been a good girl?" That's all he said. He never once noticed I was Jewish. I was safe. I was ecstatic!!! I asked for a sleepyhead doll and doll furniture, and told him I had been a very good girl all year, and would be forever and ever. I closed with an AMEN like I had heard all my Catholic friends say when they really wanted something to go well.

The night of Christmas arrived. My parents probably did a lot of research on the subject of Santa because they had the entire event worked out. Our tree was sparsely decorated. The branches cradled a few paper chains that I had made in school, a lot of silver icicles, and three strings of lights. It was a vision; a glorious dream come true. The scene was every bit of what my friends would talk about all those times when I could only listen.

There were no toys under the tree, but my Dad reassured me that Santa only comes at night when the children are asleep. The good news was that our apartment had a fireplace. The scene was set!

A favorite aunt of mine was with us that night to share my awesome experience. After dinner she asked me to take a walk with her to the candy store. As we walked hand in hand down the street, the snow started to fall. I remember thinking that it was going to be a white Christmas, and how wonderful that was for the Christians. As Christmas approached, my friends would wish on a daily basis for a snowfall on Christmas Eve. In all the pictures depicting Christ's birth there is always a snowfall, so I felt a special happiness for them that their wishes were coming true.

On the way home from Goldie's Candy and Ice Cream Shop, my wonderful aunt suddenly turned into an exuberant woman, jumping up and down and proclaiming her sighting of Santa Claus.

"Where? Where?" I shouted back at her.

"Look way up there in the sky flying through the clouds!" My aunt was shouting at the top of her lungs. "There he is! Don't you see him? He just left your house. Hurry, let's run home."

At home the toys I had asked for were there. The cookies that I had put out for Santa were gone. Before I could question Santa's early arrival, my dad piped in with an explanation. "Santa had to come here early because you and some others kids were added at the last minute to his list."

I had come this far, so I thought maybe one more request to complete the night might be granted. I asked if I could go to Midnight Mass with my friends. Mom said, "Now you've gone too far. Forget it."

The following year I found out from my friends that there is no Santa Claus. This discovery made my parents very, very happy. I became the official tree trimmer at school until I graduated. This made me very, very happy. I decided to give up my part-time Catholic notions. And that made everyone very, very happy.

All the Leaves Are Gone

Susan Lyon

This time of year a warm melancholy quietly seeps into the crisp, cool air of whispering breezes amongst the trees. My mood changes with the falling leaves when the colorful brilliance embracing us dies before our very eyes. We watch, commenting on the stark and the grey, dreading what's to come. This time of year, I miss a lot of people, places, and some things, big and small. Each fallen leaf a reminder of someone loved, now lost.

I've been helping a friend move. "What will I do without you?" I say.

"It's not like we won't see each other again," she replies. Still, she's not moving down the street. It's a big move . . . far away.

In preparation for this big move, I've seen her rearrange a perfectly lovely house and garden, staging it for the next generation of occupants. We've packed, loaded and unloaded boxes, into and out of storage, piling things upon larger things on gurneys, fitting them into seemingly impossible configurations of space.

Several times a week, I'd bike or drive or walk down my street to hers, each time cricking my neck on the fast track or stopping to gaze at another house where I once spent a lot of time as a child. It was the home of my oldest best friend.

Strangely, both houses stand mid-block, a block apart. My old friend's house looks different than it did then. The once brown-painted brick now dons a new greenish-grey façade. Or was that the house next door, I wonder? Canvassing the neighborhood, I glance down the street and back, adjusting my emotional sentiment to the changes in its architectural alignment.

Each time I pass it now, a different memory emerges. I once knew the names of the neighbors who lived in those houses on the street and the kids who played with her brother across it. We had a crush on the boy in the grey house with shutters and in the large, dirty-white stucco a few doors down.

The names flow with stops and starts around my stressed memory as my older physical self passes by. My childhood friend and I shared so much life together: stories, secrets, activities, school and church school. I knew the tales of all her Southern relatives (how her grandfather refused to kiss her mother goodbye in Memphis when she marched for civil rights with Martin Luther King) and she knew mine. I played with her sisters, too. They were not "playdates" easily dispensed one for another. We were all friends. We were family.

Both of us loved to walk home from school "the long way" so we could talk and talk and talk about what, I can guess, but not recall. There were overnights, chattering late into the night—reprimanded by our parents and paid in lethargy the next midday.

The two of us were always together somehow, somewhere. She and her family were a constant, taken-for-granted presence of comfort, love, security and well-being.

She's gone now. The family left years ago. The house has changed owners several times over. Yet her memory, still chiseled in the bricks that hold its walls together, represent the boyfriends, work, trials, travels, marriage, friends, children, separations and distance, places endured and enjoyed—all things shared—that built a life no longer there.

My rock-solid, childhood friend is gone for good. She died. I still can't believe she's gone. Nor can I believe in the permanency of it either.

So many losses cry out as I pass these old, renewed and new houses. Their silent shouts echo from within: a stranger in familiar territory, living on the edges of an outer world. *It's as though your life has been erased,* someone once told me.

And so my contemporary, emptying her home of many years, only adds to feeling pushed toward the margins of an inexplicable void, while the whispering melancholy of fall, in all its bright and glorious splendor, mockingly seeps deep into my soul.

Family Lore

Reflections in Black and White

Ann Fiegen

My mother's sadness owned her. She was unhappy with her life, with her marriage, and often with me. Longing for what she felt she had missed, she took no pleasure in what she had. "I gave up my life for you" was one of her favorite things to say to me. Every day of every year that I remember my mother was sad, and her sadness filled our house overshadowing any joy that dared be present.

On a rainy fall morning in 2000, she died. The years preceding were painful for us both. For her because she was devastatingly unhappy and sick. For me, her only child, there were times when I felt so consumed by my solitary responsibility for her care that I couldn't breathe. My years with her were a struggle, and when she died I took a deep breath and for the first time thought I might begin to be free of the angst that was tightly woven into the volatile relationship that we had shared for so long.

As eternal victim, my mother believed that all she did was give, but the reality was quite the opposite. She took. She robbed people of happiness to make herself happy, of self-esteem to make her feel better about herself, of optimism to support her belief that there really was no hope. She often referred to herself as a "loner" as if that were something to be proud of. The standard she set for others was so high that no one survived it. She had no close friends, no contact with family members other than me, and once I ceased being that child who needed her absolutely, loved her unconditionally, and agreed with her unfailingly, I, too, fell short of eliciting her praise or feeling like a recipient of her love.

Not long ago, while packing for a move, I came across a box marked in my mother's hand with my name followed by "the good years." I had taken it with me when she died but could never bring myself to open it for fear that my mother's representations of "the good years" would not necessarily be good for me. The time had come to open the box and decide what if anything of its contents was worth taking with me to my new home. The tape separated easily and I was initially relieved to discover only the usual memorabilia—report cards, notes, some of my school artwork, and a baby blanket that I assume had been mine. At the bottom was a small book of collected love poems that held between its pages an old black-and-white Polaroid photo of my mother and me. In it I am probably four or five. I sit on her lap and we look at one another rather than at the camera. Time has aged the picture and diminished its clarity, but the bond between its two subjects is disarmingly clear. The love is palpable, and there is joy.

I wondered if she had seen in the photo what I saw and saved it because of its visual image of "the good years," or if the book and its contents just happened to be in the bottom of the box she chose for her memorabilia. Impossible to know for sure, but I do know that there are no accidents. We all are given moments of epiphany that have the potential to change our lives. Change us in ways that can make us better people, happier people, kinder people. Finding the picture gave me such a moment, and I grabbed it recognizing the possibility to allow myself to remember my mother with more kindness and less judgment. Since that time I have created a mental "good years" box of my own, and filled it with memories of my mother that were indeed good. Memories from those early years when I was still the child she always wanted.

I have remembered our apartment filled with the mouth-watering aromas of her dinner preparations. I have never enjoyed a meal more than those she created on a stove with legs in a small apartment kitchen on Chicago's West Side. There were homemade noodles that she rolled and hung on the back of a kitchen chair to dry, finger dumplings with pork and sauerkraut, breakfast crepes with sour cream, strawberries and brown sugar, spaghetti sauce that had simmered for hours with her "special" meatballs, garlic bread and fresh grated parmesan cheese, meatloaf with mashed potatoes and asparagus, lamb chops with mint jelly, and, her *piece de resistance*, apple pie with melt-in-your-mouth crust, still warm from the oven. It was she who laid the groundwork for the inveterate foodie that I am, for my interest in cooking, my love of eating, and my insatiable need to cook for those I love.

I sometimes still see her lovely face reflected in the bathroom mirror as the little girl me sat on the sink watching her glorious features come alive with Revlon Cherries in the Snow lipstick and Maybelline sable brown mascara applied to her lashes with water and a tiny red brush. Her flawless beauty was as simple as light makeup and a Colgate smile, and her sense of style was impeccable. She instilled in me the importance of looking my best. For me, there was never any question about for whom I dressed to please. It was never for men, other women, or myself. It was always for my mother.

Recalling her love for the big screen, I have felt her sitting next to me sharing buttered popcorn and Milk Duds in neighborhood movie theaters that were palace-like structures with names like The Marbro and the Paradise. Their huge marble lobbies were guarded by towering statues of the gods, and their lavishly ornate restrooms inspired make believe. Together we watched as Cary Grant, John Wayne, Gary Cooper, Judy Garland, Doris Day and Susan Hayward sang, danced and galloped their way into our hearts. My mother's love for the movies was contagious; I love them too, and it was she who taught me how.

My mother also loved music and was enchanted by musical talent of any kind. On a very limited budget, she made sure she found a way for me to take piano lessons, voice lessons and dance lessons. She bought a Kimball spinet piano on time payments and squeezed it into our tiny apartment so that I could practice at home. She played scratchy old Caruso records that had belonged to my grandmother at high volume on an old record player in the dining room. The sound of his voice became as familiar to me as those of the pop artists of my generation. And the crooners— she loved them all—Frank Sinatra, Tony Bennett, Vic Damone, Dean Martin, Nat King Cole. I heard them so often that I knew the words to all their love songs. Still do. For all of my adult life I have been singularly moved, often to tears, by musical talent, and transported by the power of music to a place reserved for those who share my passion. My love for music has sustained me, inspired me, and brought me happiness beyond measure. This love was a gift from my mother.

I have remembered her as the smart one. It was she who helped me with my homework, handled the finances, did the taxes and wrote the notes to the nuns. She could spell all the hard words and use them in sentences. She worked crossword puzzles in ink. If there were ever a medical question, she probably had the answer; and to me, most important of all, she knew the details of the personal lives of the stars. Whenever my father said, "Good thing you got your mother's brains," I knew he was right and had a moment of gratitude.

And, in the end, I have seen a certain positive legacy in what I had only viewed as the ways in which I felt my mother had failed me. When I held each of my sons in my arms for the first time, I whispered a silent promise that I would do my best to be the finest mother I could be. I have strived to give them my support when they needed it, celebrate their successes, and commiserate with them over their disappointments. I love them without condition, and often tell them how much. Every time I succeeded in being the mother I wished I had had, it is in a way because of my mother.

I don't know what I think about heaven. If indeed there is another place where our spirits go when we die, I hope that she is surrounded by peace, and joy, and love. I hope that it smells like apple pie there, that Caruso is singing and that there are flocks of city birds for her to feed. As for me, I hope that the anger that for so long was my constant companion will continue to diminish. And for those times when I feel myself falling from grace, I hope that I am within arm's reach of that faded Polaroid and the love that it reflects.

Motherhood

Fumiko Tokunaga Jensen

"I hate motherhood," I lamented. My friend Marianne chuckled on the other side of the phone. She knows exactly what I am talking about. She and I worry too much about our grown children. We both have a boy and a girl in their twenties and we often lend each other a shoulder to cry on. On many sleepless nights, I think about them—if they are going to have a happy life or whether maybe they need hardship to grow up. Most importantly, I worry that if they can't develop their many talents they might end up having unfulfilled lives?

"Please don't worry about us," they often beg me. I understand that they want to be free. They don't want to feel burdened with their mother's worries. When I was young, did I think about my mother's worries? No. I did exactly what I wanted to do.

Before I accidentally got pregnant with our son, I used to declare that I would never have babies. I wanted to be free to move around the world. Besides, I was never interested in changing diapers. I was not interested in babies at all. Period. But four months into my pregnancy, when morning sickness started to ease, not only did I feel physically energetic, I found myself filled with a deep peace.

My husband and I were living in New York City then and we did not have health insurance. I would have to go either to Japan, my country, or to Denmark, my husband's country, to deliver the baby. Because my musician husband had several concerts in Denmark during the time the baby was due, we decided to do it in Denmark.

In the seventh month of my pregnancy, I was on the plane to Denmark by myself because my husband was working in New York. But I did not feel alone. When the plane jolted, I talked to the baby, saying, "Do not worry. I am with you."

My husband arrived in mid-May, the most beautiful time of the year. The peaceful summer days were long. It never got completely dark. My in-laws had a farm and one of their five horses was pregnant, too. One late afternoon, the colt was born. It was lying on the earth. When his mother finished licking the placenta, the colt tried to stand up with its wobbly legs and fell to the ground. But the second time, he succeeded in standing up and snuggled up to his mother.

That night, I went into labor. At three o'clock in the morning, my husband drove me to the hospital, 20 kilometers from the farm. The sun was already high; the earth was filled with soft sunlight.

Around five o'clock in the morning, our son was born. I don't remember the pain, but the feeling of ectasy after birth surprised me. I had never experienced being high. Drugs always gave me a headache or made me dizzy, but this must be the feeling, I thought. The baby didn't open his eyes until the next morning. When I saw that pair of eyes, a light was turned on deep inside me that I felt would give warmth deep within forever.

Back in New York, we lived on West 42nd Street. New York City was a dangerous place back in the late '70s and '80s. I tied the baby fast with a snuggly and a backpack filled with a bottle and diapers. I walked between drug dealers and homeless people sleeping on the street and went to the different museums: the Met, the Frick Collection and the Guggenheim.

Sometimes he fell asleep. When he was hungry, I gave him a bottle. I was no longer afraid of walking around on the streets of New York. I thought "I am a mother. I am strong. I will save my baby from anything." And I finally felt grown up.

Several years later, I had the good fortune to have a baby girl. I have observed my children in wonder. I admired their pureness, their absolutely non-judgmental view of the world. Every second I spent with them was eye opening. In hindsight, I am not sure I was a good mother, as I may have enjoyed them too much.

And now that they grew up and left home, I can't stop worrying about them.

Change of Seasons

Ruth Sterlin

"Run, Jamma!" My four-year-old granddaughter pulls me by the hand, running uphill and laughing, the spring wind blowing back her sandy brown hair to show off her rarely seen forehead. *Jamma* has been my nickname since Finnie's older sister was two and couldn't pronounce "Grandma." Finnie is always in motion and eases playfully through her own space. I struggle to keep up with her.

As we make our way up the hill, Finnie points authoritatively at everything from robins to crocuses to sidewalk slugs, knowing my eyes will follow her finger and share her wonder. We both kneel down to examine winter's leftovers, a latticework of veins in the fallen leaves, stripped of their greenery by the cold of winter and leaving behind a large blanket of lace to cover the wet ground.

Suddenly, Finnie spies a hole the size of her fist in the trunk of an enormous fir tree. Inside, a hairy black spider lounges comfortably in its web, although not for long. Finnie digs into nature's leftovers at the bottom of the tree and finds a twig perfect for invading the spider's home. Carefully, she lifts the spider on to her twig, web and all. She examines it suspiciously, as it is now shrouded in its own web. When it begins moving as if to free itself, she quickly wipes the whole tangle off of her twig using the ground as her rag, Finnie's form of spring cleaning in a world she has claimed as her own.

Continuing our walk uphill, we talk about the light rain, which is ever present in northwest Washington, the toys on various porches we pass, and what Finnie wants for lunch when we get back home. She giggles at two squirrels chasing each other from tree to tree until one of them drops to the ground. Then she spots a hawk.

"What's that?" she asks, her finger following the arc of its flight through the sky.

"A hawk! Look how wide it can spread its wings!" I answer.

Our eyes stay glued to its smooth movement as it rides the wind. Then suddenly, a passing car intrudes on our moment, its wheels spinning through a deep puddle, soaking our jackets and making us laugh as we wipe ourselves off. The unplanned shower causes us both to rethink how far we want to go.

"This is a long walk. I'm tired," says Finnie.

"Let's sit down and rest," I say. Feeling a wet chill building inside of me, I'm relieved that she may be ready to end our walk. I pray that she won't ask for a piggy-back ride, as she often does. Finnie finds us a soft carpet of pine needles under a tree. I place my hesitating bottom on the moist ground just in time for her to plop into my lap, lean against me, and put her legs on top of mine. The tree supports us both. As I hold her, I look at her pink gym shoes and think back to the tiny footprints her feet made when she was just one day old.

The visiting nurse had come to the house to check on the newborn and had put Finnie's tiny feet onto an inkpad and then placed them on paper. During the nurse's visit, my daughter Miriam sat in an armchair, her eyes puffy from lack of sleep. To give her a break, I took the crying baby into my arms. I remember how Finnie's whole body fit between my palm and my elbow. Now, as Finnie sits in my lap, her body extends from my shins all the way to my chin. She is growing before my eyes at the same time that I am shrinking.

As we sit quietly under our tree, Finnie's finger follows the protruding veins on the surface of my hand as if she were reading a map and deciding which road to take. She discovers that she can move one particularly large vein back and forth, and this makes her giggle.

"Why does it do that?" she asks. I start to laugh too, trying to be a good sport about the swelling of my aging veins.

"Well, as we get older, our veins get bigger and sometimes they have to poke their heads out."

In silence, I feel an overwhelming tenderness towards Finnie. It surrounds us, hanging in the air like the smell of the freshly baked bread we had for breakfast. I also have a dawning realization that the moisture from our carpet is gradually seeping into my pants.

"How about let's head for home," I venture. Finnie leaps to her feet, and by the time I have worked myself into a standing position, she's already halfway down the hill. "WAIT!" I shout, and she stops and turns around. While she waits, she picks up a long branch and begins to dance around with it. Then she strikes it on the ground several times. Apparently it meets with her approval, because she keeps it by her side. By then I've caught up with her and we continue on down the road. Hand-in-hand, I feel our worlds overlap, in spite of the fact that we are at such different places in life. Finnie holds her trophy branch high and struts proudly forward. As we approach the house, I let her go ahead of me, which she does using the branch as a walking stick. Watching from behind, I see her increase her stride—as if enlarging the space of her world—and wonder how long I'll inhabit mine. She turns to wave at me and then runs the rest of the way home, stick in hand, knowing that I will follow.

Paternal Duties

Susan E. Cohen

Who will give me away?
With my father long buried
There's no one quite right for the part.
There is, of course,
My candy store uncle from New Jersey
With similar genes
But still not my father
And the scholar who advises me
On getting ahead and other worldly matters
But still not my father.
And all the benign older male strangers
I briefly adopt from time to time
And none of them my father.

No, my father's the one
Who reminds you not to walk
With your hands in your pockets
Cause he broke a leg once like that.
And not to lose your head
And do things in too much of a hurry

And always to notice
Where all the fire exits are.
There were certainly a lot of teachings
He gave out early
Which turned out to be just in time
For me to have to grow up without him.

My father, with the soft heart,
Always warning me not to trust people
Like he made a practice of doing.
Couldn't that man be allowed
To descend for just one hour
And march me up and down
And back and forth across the aisle?
Beaming this, this is my daughter
Whom I sired and raised
As long as I could.

Oh, he'd be busy all right
Sternly appraising the groom
And noticing how much I've grown up
And listening with approval
As the glass smashed.

And then, if God were feeling
Particularly expansive,
My father would get to stay
For a dance or two,

Like at other people's weddings
Where they announce
"And now a dance
For Daddy and his little girl"
And I sit there cringing
At their maudlin sentiment
And their not knowing what it is
To not have someone around
To rebel against
And to advise you
While you pretend you have no interest
And couldn't care less what he says.

You see, we'd be there
Out on the dance floor
Moving in perfect harmony—
A fine sight for all the daughters
Arguing with their living dads.

But as it is,
I'll have to walk solo
Remembering how my father
Used to run alongside my bicycle
Long after it was really necessary
Holding a few token fingers
On the handlebars and frame
Knowing before I did
That I could balance by myself.

Forever Aftering

Ann Fiegen

On that Thursday morning, as with most Thursday mornings, I was in my kitchen watering the plants. That room, bathed in morning sunlight, was my sacred space. It hosted a variety of growing things, all of which I tended to religiously, loving the fact that I was able to keep them flourishing. The most spectacular plant in the room was a Boston fern whose bright green fronds spanned the entire width of the window above which it hung. I often spoke to that plant, misted it regularly, and dosed it with plant food whenever its green became a little less vibrant. It was perfection, and I took great pride in my nurturing skills.

The radio was on, and as I poured the plant a soaking drink, a German psychologist known as Dr. Ruth was taking calls from listeners who had questions about their sex lives. Small but mighty, what she lacked in stature, Dr. Ruth made up for in chutzpah. At a time when it was not a matter for public discussion, she spoke openly about human sexuality. No topic was too indelicate, no question was left unanswered.

There were a couple of callers asking the usual questions involving premature ejaculation, impotence and female orgasm, and then came a call from a listener who suspected her husband might be gay. She sounded nervous and more than a little embarrassed to ask the question, but Dr. Ruth didn't miss a beat. With her characteristic accent, she replied, "My Dahlink, ven you even sink your husband is gay, he is gay." And with that simple exchange, the question that had owned the back of my mind for so long was answered, and I knew my life would never be the same.

It was a freeze frame moment for me. Everything around me stopped, and I stood, watering can in hand amid all my green perfection, staring out the window.

What the hell do I do now?

During the weeks that followed, I vacillated between not eating and being unable to stop, sleeping all the time and not sleeping at all, racing through days like a whirling dervish and vegging mindlessly on the couch. I bottomed out in September. The kids were back in school, and I still had more questions than answers. Abjectly paralyzed, I simply went to bed and there I stayed, in my place of sanctuary, where I wasn't afraid, where nothing had to change. Outside the sanctuary were confusion, hard decisions, and a life so altered that I had no idea how to live it. And so, in bed I remained, calmed by the sameness and predictability of each day. My husband filled in the empty spaces as best he could, silently hoping that the next day would be different.

Friends, family and co-workers began to worry about me. Sometimes I'd take their calls and go on about my mystery virus and its debilitating effects on my energy level. I told the same story at work and tapped into my unused sick days. My kids came in periodically lingering only as long as it took to provide CliffsNotes versions of their days, and then leaving to resume their places in the comfort zone of the life that was going on outside my four walls. I don't know how many days went by. Five? A week?

Finally there came the morning that I began to fear that my retreat from life would jeopardize my being a fit mother. And so, I rose from my self-imposed coma and resumed my place among the living. My mantra became one goal a day, and I pretty much stuck to it, consistently moving towards shaping a new reality, one in which our broken family could regroup with the least amount of trauma and emotional pain.

In 1981, gay was something Rock Hudson was still pretending not to be, and coming out was what young society debutantes did in white dresses at cotillions. My mother thought Liberace was sexy, for God's sake. My hairstylist was gay, as was the bartender at the private club where I worked, but my husband? Whose husband was gay? No one I had even heard of, but the truth was that while I had been married to my first love for seventeen years, it was all irreparably wrong because I was a woman, and he was a gay man. My husband was gay, the ultimate irreconcilable difference. And so, I filed for divorce and we moved forward, because there was nothing else to do, no other choice that could be made.

Divorce is a grueling process. There were lawyers, custody arrangements, financial decisions—all of which required answers before the court date that loomed in our future. Times were different then, and for my strictly Catholic-born-and-bred husband to admit that he was gay to anyone, even himself, was impossible. I was convinced our then-teenaged sons needed to be protected from a truth that might be damaging to their relationship with their father and add confusion to their own emerging sexualities. I was not interested in "outing" him. The charade needed to be maintained in order for us all to emerge less scarred. And so, we moved through divorce proceedings with neither of us ever even whispering to anyone the truth that had shattered life as we knew it.

It was a painful journey. There was anger, hurt, and great sadness. We wrestled with constructing the best new reality for our sons, eventually working out a shared custody agreement where he and I moved in and out of our home and an apartment we shared at six-month intervals. This allowed our boys' lives to remain relatively constant and provided us both with a continuing live-in relationship with them. With sheer determination we maintained our arrangement for six years until our youngest son was out of high school, at which point my husband and I each took a deep breath and moved toward yet another new reality, one in which our contact with one another was minimal, polite if not gracious.

Disconnects have always been ridiculously hard for me. I tend to attach and hang on for dear life, and my connection with my former husband was no exception to that tendency. The experiences we had shared were life-defining, and the conjoined hopes and dreams of our very young selves bound us with ties that were not easy to sever. Eventually, however, with time, the great healer, we were able to move on, and there were many years when we had no contact at all aside from events related to our children and eventually to our grandchildren.

Even time, however, could not erase all that we had once shared: his working three jobs to keep us afloat on a teacher's salary for those few years when I needed to stay at home with babies; the boys' birthday parties, sporting events, pinewood derbies and Halloween costumes; the sleepless nights holding feverish bodies or comforting after bad dreams; that time of dancing together smoothly and easily in step and in tune to the music of life as a family.

Several years ago my former husband and I were seated next to one another at our grand baby's birthday party and we began to reconnect. For the first time since our divorce, our conversation wasn't strained. Perhaps the wine helped, but when he made me laugh, I remembered how funny he was. During our discussion of a book we had both recently read, I remembered how smart he was. The commonality that had once brought us together was working again, and we settled into a comfortable place that we both enjoyed. Why wouldn't we? We were still the same people who had once promised to love one another forever. And so, in the months that followed, we tested the waters of yet another reality. We became friends.

Now we're in a place where we do together the things that old friends do. We go to the movies, see a play, call and text one another to share a laugh or concern. We meet friends for lunch or dinner and discuss old times, current events, the beauty and brilliance of our grandchildren, and the hilarious/tragic issues of these, our "Golden Years."

Strange but kind of nice, really, to be actively involved with this man with whom I spent so much of my past. Yes, in a way I am kind of dating my former husband who happens to be gay, but times have changed. We have changed. Thankfully, maturity has given us the wisdom to know how important it is to nurture all connections of the heart like Boston ferns allowing them to flourish rather than destroying them with anger and resentment . . . to know that love does indeed endure if we allow for its own form of limited perfection.

Life is so full of surprises, bends in the road, unanticipated outcomes that catch all of us off-guard and open doors we thought were shut forever. I have never totally abandoned my belief in fairy tales. And now I bask in the knowledge that in life, as in every fairy tale, there is always the possibility of a happy ending and that these happy endings are as diverse as the tales they close. After so many decades of believing that my forever after had been denied, I now know for sure that I was wrong. On the contrary, it was granted. Forever afters just don't always look the same.

A War by Any Other Name

Ruth Sterlin

During his senior year of college, our son Sam announced that he was going to join the Air Force. We were having dinner and I choked on my chicken, coughing so hard I could barely hear him. I didn't really want to hear him, being the product of a long line of antimilitarists.

In time, I was able to calm down and actually listen to what he was trying to tell my husband and me. From that point on, I learned a lot about who Sam is and how he is shaping his life with great thoughtfulness. He explained that his decision to join the Air Force was his way of caring about others and giving back to his country. Who would have ever thought . . . ?

As luck would have it, ten years later, our son volunteered to go to Afghanistan for a year to help train the Afghani Air Force. I was dumbstruck by this decision and spent that whole year having sleepless nights, worrying about how long his luck would hold out in a war zone.

One day, eyes on the road, driving home from yoga class, I happened to turn on the news.

" . . . eight U.S. Air Force pilots and one other American have been shot and killed at Kabul International Airport." The air base where my son Sam was stationed. I stopped breathing and things began to move in slow-motion. I don't even remember making it home and walking through the door.

"David! DAVID!" I screamed as I looked for my husband.

"He's okay! Sam's okay!" my husband yelled from the basement, crying with relief. Sam had reached him by phone to let us know that he was safe. David and I held each other before I sank tearfully into the couch. Sam called back later in the day, not allowed to reveal many details of what had taken place, and I could hear the pain in his voice. During the shooting, he was working on a plane at the other end of the airport. The gunman hadn't found him. The other nine weren't so lucky, and Sam lost nine co-workers, including his close friend Jeffrey Ausborn. As a team, they were serving as part of the NATO force assigned to train pilots in the Afghani Air Force.

This tragedy was reported on CNN as "a small firearms incident." A small firearms incident! It wasn't small to Sam as he walked in the procession of caskets towards the transport plane that would bring them home. It wasn't small to Jeffrey's Ausborn's wife either.

When Sam departed for "the Stan," I told myself that he would be safe. How dangerous could it be to train Afghani pilots? After the shooting, I often stood at our picture window, staring at the yellow ribbons I had hung around each of our trees. Seeing the ribbon ends flap in the wind always made me think of flypaper strips trying to shake off tiny winged corpses of the flies that had flown into them. I would ask myself, *why are we in this war?*

In grade school, Sam used to complain about his hair. He was convinced that its honey color attracted bees, and when they buzzed around him, he would run away from them swatting the air. I told him that the bees followed him because he was so sweet. "Mo-om," he would parry, making the word into two syllables, "cut it out!" No more bees now, just the ear-splitting buzz of the C-130 he flies as its nose lifts into the air. I remember when he couldn't even find his socks. How did he learn to fly?

During his entire deployment in Afghanistan, we had a Blue Star Banner hanging in our front door window. The banner came to us through the mail, courtesy of the U.S. Government. It felt like an unpleasant reminder that our family had a military member serving in harm's way. While Sam was in Afghanistan, neighbors would stop at our door and ask,

"What's this flag on your door?"

Being military parents is a lonely business, especially in the suburb where we live. To this day, I am still amazed at how many of our neighbors don't know that the blue star is a symbol signifying that a family has a military member in a war or danger zone. Most of our neighbors' upper-middle-class sons and daughters are busy going to grad school and moving into lucrative careers. I am also struck by the easy acceptance my friends have of *other* people's kids being sent off to battle, *you know, the ones without much education who can't really find jobs anyway.* When my anger reaches a bursting point, I picture myself standing in the middle of the street, red-faced, yelling,

"THAT'S RIGHT! SOMEONE ELSE'S BABIES WILL DO OUR COUNTRY'S DIRTY WORK. Someone else's babies will get to flip a coin in these wars. *Heads,* you get traumatic brain injury! *Tails,* you get your ass blown off!"

Sam has taught me a lot about determination. The tragedy of 9/11 occurred right after he joined the Air Force. While we were all shaking in our boots, Sam was not deterred. As a Second Lieutenant, he decided to apply for pilot training. Believe me when I say that he would not take *no* for an answer. (That hasn't changed since he was two.) The Air Force turned down his pilot training application—not once, but *twice*. Instead of feeling discouraged, he tried harder. His passion for flying and his perseverance to get into the program was unbelievable. For three years, Sam clutched dead-nuts-on to his goal until it finally happened. He got the phone call telling him he was in!

Happy as a clam that he had been accepted into pilot training, he came home to prepare. In no time at all, our basement floor was piled high with old grade school papers, clay sculptures, drawings, report cards, a large remote control airplane he'd made in high school, and a collection of socks (he can find them now). All trash-bound! Sam pared down his possessions as if he were a rocket trimming smooth in order to hug its path after take-off. Fearing what might lurk ahead, I cried like a baby.

"Mom, can you at least wait until it's time for me to go before you fall apart?" Poor guy. For his sake, I tried to pull myself together.

Since then, my husband and I have attended as many of our son's military ceremonies as possible. Numerous times, I heard Sam's entire squadron pledge their loyalty, respect and superior conduct in the fight against "all enemies foreign and domestic," the words whizzing through the air like bullets.

At Sam's official Air Force winging ceremony, he looked so proud to be a pilot. Finally! The day started with a celebration coffee and a speech by the Commanding Officer. He told all of us that these pilots—our sons and daughters—were readying themselves "to go into harm's way." After the coffee, my husband and I pinned Sam's wings to his uniform and had our picture taken together. Then the squadron chanted the usual loyalty pledge. It was then that I realized for the first time that my son was promising, if

necessary, to make *"the ultimate sacrifice."* Three little words. They reverber-
ated through my sudden hollowness like the tolling of a giant bell.

Friends were very supportive after Sam left for the Stan, ready with a
hug whenever I needed one. Inevitably, though, they asked the question,

"How can you stand knowing that Sam is in Afghanistan?"

How can I cope with the fact that one day my son is in a safe place,
and the next day he's in the middle of a war? My friends meant well, but
they could never really understand. Blue Star Mothers and Fathers are the
only ones who really get it. We cope because we have no choice. Because
having a nervous breakdown is not going to help our babies out there in
the middle of this catastrophe that no one will even call a *war.*

Every time I remember Sam's pledge of *the ultimate sacrifice*, I am
plagued by a sense that our children—out there in the middle of dust,
roadside bombs and deadly chaos—are *way too alone!* They're holed up in
powder kegs all over the Middle East, southern Asia, and Africa wondering every single day if a fuse will ignite and blow them to smithereens.
And yet, it's second-page news.

Where is everybody! Who besides the one percent of our children
who are in the military is making sacrifices for these far-away wars that no
one will even call *wars?* Why was it so hard to find real information about
the Kabul shooting which should have been in the front page headlines?
For several years now, the PBS News Hour has been among the few news
shows to have special moments of silence for the Honor Roll of American
Service Personnel Killed in the Iraq and Afghanistan Conflicts—other
places as well. And we are left with a parade of young faces who stare at
us through silent eyes.

During Sam's entire Afghanistan assignment, I would often sit at my
kitchen table, terrified every time my doorbell rang. I didn't sleep well, and

I frequently felt depressed. I'm still waiting for the answer to my original question, *Why are we in these wars?* Over the past few years, my question has broadened to include a general questioning of the stunningly misguided U.S. Government actions all over the Middle East and southern Asia.

So far, I've been one of the lucky Blue Star Mothers and Fathers. While thousands of soldiers have died, Sam has returned home safely from all of his deployments. The last stop of his military career will be at the Airbase in Little Rock, Arkansas, where he will once again be a pilot trainer. Sounds pretty safe . . . unless . . . well, unless he gets deployed again to some God-forsaken place of danger. That possibility? I try not to think about it.

Painfully Funny

My Favorite Skirt

Fumiko Tokunaga Jensen

I bought the skirt in Harajuku, Tokyo. If you are a so-called fashionista, you might have heard about the name of this neighborhood. Harajuku is a fashionable neighborhood in the middle of Tokyo. The young woman with a heavily pierced face, who used to cut my hair in Chicago, often asked me about Harajuku and told me that she hoped to go there one day. She told me about a popular singer who sings about the place.

There are several expensive stores like Chanel, Dolce Gabana, Dior and St. Laurent into which I would never step. But Harajuku is most famous for wild and crazy fashion for young people. One of the side streets of this neighborhood, "Takeshita cyo," is crowded with youth who are dressed as if it is a Halloween parade. It is the kind of unique and extreme style out of which new fashion trends are born. I had heard that some world-famous designers have drawn inspiration from that street of Harajuku.

I sometimes go there to find performance clothing for outdoor summer concerts when I play the piano. My older sister, who accompanies me shopping, shakes her head and complains that I should shop at stores more suitable for my age. But I found a skirt there that I liked very much. It was made of dark brown, transparent fabric with a large butterfly, a swirly design of flowers and several small shining stones. The layer underneath was a silky deep brown petticoat.

I thought this skirt would look good on stage. My sister made a little grimace of disgust as if she gave up on me and said, "Your fashion sense is……." She meant "terrible," but didn't say that. It didn't hurt my feelings, though, because in my opinion, her fashion sense is rather dull. I didn't say a word. I just smiled. After many years of experience I learned I should never criticize her, in order to keep our relationship intact. The hierarchy is strict between older and younger sisters.

On the concert stage the following summer, the skirt was a hit, especially among young women and teenage girls. They said, it was "cool" or "awesome" or "beautiful" and asked where I bought it. I was pleased with my "fashion sense." I smiled to myself as I wondered what my older sister would think now.

I wore the skirt for three concert seasons. One evening, just before a concert as I was waiting back stage, I noticed that the elastic waistband of the petticoat was loose. I didn't have time to change and assumed it would surely last through the concert.

The cellist whom I was accompanying and I entered the stage to a glaring light and an enthusiastically applauding audience. In the middle of the stage, I suddenly stopped walking. I couldn't move my feet. I looked down and to my horror, I saw the petticoat had fallen and was around my ankles. While the cellist was bowing toward the audience, I walked as quickly as possible with gliding steps to the piano bench.

As soon as I sat down on the bench, I pulled the petticoat quickly off and shoved it towards my page-turner who was sitting next to me. His name was Tristan, a young Canadian with shoulder-length wavy hair, white long pianist fingers and a romantic Chopinesque air about him. He looked confused as something soft and dark brown was thrown onto his lap without any explanation.

The cellist and I started to play Prokofieff's "Symphony Concertante." During the first movement, I didn't know what I was playing. I was blushing with embarrassment. At the same time I was having a hard time holding back from bursting out laughing. I was also anxiously trying to figure out how I would exit after the performance. But when I began the second movement, I told myself to focus and I managed to concentrate through the rest of the piece. When we finished, I held the music in front of me and walked backwards through the door to the backstage area.

Because the color of the skirt was dark despite being transparent and the stage light was above my head instead of behind me, fortunately no one noticed the incident. Although the people who are close to me were wondering, "Why is she behaving weird tonight?"

I was glad that my sister was not there.

Is There a G-d . . . or Does Stuff Just Happen?

Trudi Goodman

I don't believe there is a God. I always doubted it, but there was a time just a few years ago when I experienced the clincher. It was Rosh Hashana. I was shopping and not being respectful to the observance of the holiday. "I will probably be punished." I thought. The logical side of me responded, "Are you crazy? How would God, if indeed there is one, find you among the seven billion people on earth?"

While walking through the mall I tried to ignore the eyes of all the non-Jewish shoppers. I imagined their scary words, and who hasn't heard them before? "God will punish you." "But I feel safe because I don't believe in God." I wise-cracked back to this voice in my head. But just in case, I added, "It's in God's hands." And just like the magician when he pulls out a rabbit from his black hat, my mind uncovered another thought . . . "There but for the grace of God go I."

Daydreaming on my guilt trip, I hardly noticed that my face had become too close to the sidewalk outside the department store. My screams caught my attention and the cloud my head was in disappeared. My eyes were closed, but I could hear a lot of O.M.G.s. I also thought I might have heard whispers of . . . "She's a sinner."

The paramedics carried me on a stretcher to an ambulance. The crowd was thickening around me when a nervy woman in the middle of the crowd shouted out her intentions.

"I'll get in touch with your sister and tell her to go to the hospital. The paramedic said they were taking you to Skokie Rush North Shore."

O.M.G., the voice belonged to my sister's sister-in-law, who was standing in the crowd holding her shopping bags...another sinner.

"I would really appreciate it if you called nobody. Thank you!"

On the way to the hospital I begged the paramedic to give me an assessment. He told me that my blood pressure was 180 over whatever, but that anything else is hard to know without an X-ray. I didn't like this answer, so I kept arguing in favor of a bruise or two diagnosis. I finally realized I was debating with myself. The paramedic knew not to answer the ravings of a madwoman, even when I said I was responsible for bringing the vegetables to the holiday dinner. I should have known better. He knew nothing about a Jewish holiday.

In the Emergency Room all those details my mother had filled my head with came rushing back. "JUST IN CASE you're in an accident" read like an important document in my brain and took over. I got a grip and the seriousness of JUST IN CASE trumped my pain. That list of how to be prepared ahead of time for the unexpected became my focus.

Because of the holiday I was wearing my recently purchased underpants. They were blue, a friendly shade of blue. Always wear clean, no-holes underwear. You never know, JUST IN CASE. Be sure you are bathed and legs shaved. A pedicure wouldn't hurt. Had I missed anything in my preparation for JUST IN CASE? Too late if I did. I'll try not to be embarrassed.

The leaning-over-me group of white coats began to annoy me. This was silly and I told them so. It was all a waste of time. No, I don't think I need a tetanus shot. Yes, my last one was less than ten years ago, maybe. And then, adding insult to injury, in walks my sister. The informant had reached her. After her big hello, there were words of comfort.

"O.M.G., it could have been worse. You could have broken a hip, or your neck, or your back!"

After all her could-haves, she whipped out from her purse a bottle of eye drops, grabbed my face, and while the nurse was undressing me, proceeded to put drops in my eyes. "Your eyes are so bloodshot," she tells me. Never mind my face is bleeding, and chunks of skin are missing in places. I thought for sure she was going to put lipstick on me. At this point I was willing to call upon a God, any God, to please help me. I'll do anything. I'll go to Temple every chance I get. Please, God, help me out here.

My sister loves to remind me when I need lipstick or some color on my face. Looking good under any circumstances is her highest priority. An aide arrived to take me to X-ray. Was this God intervening? Did he send a messenger? As I was wheeled out of the Emergency Room on a gurney, my sister informed me that her son the lawyer was on top of it. The lawsuit was in process. And from a distance, I heard her say, "You need the money."

I had to wait four days before I could have the surgery required to repair the damage done to my shattered knee. I don't like being put to sleep. Truth is, I'm terrified. If I'm not awake, how can I be sure I'm still here? All my friends and family members told me they would pray for me. They were all going to ask God to pay special attention to me. I've told them on several occasions there's no logic to the existence of God, but just in case I was wrong, I told them to do what they thought was best. The surgery was a success because I woke up! I compare the experience to the many times after a plane trip when I'm surprised that we didn't crash.

I left the hospital on the same day after the surgery to begin a year of recovery. I was haunted by the memory of the tetanus shot I refused to take. What if I was wrong? Now I had to live with the possibility of Tetanus. Every day I moved my jaw in all directions. Finally, two weeks later, I declared myself physically healthy, but totally insane! Every day of my recovery I relived my accident wondering why it happened. Being punished? Maybe, but doubtful.

If there is a God, I would certainly hope that he/she is paying attention to the issues that are important to all mankind. And it wouldn't hurt if he/she was blessed with a good sense of humor.

Odd Attachments

By Ann Fiegen

There was a time when I thought my eccentricities were normal. I blithely assumed that everyone felt the same attachments to inanimate objects that I did, and pretty much didn't give it another thought. Until, that is, the day when a friend suggested I get rid of a mirror that hung in my front hall. She meant well and spoke the truth when she said it was not very attractive and too big for the space, but I reacted immediately with a firm *No!* I explained to her that I believed that mirrors, in some magical place, held the images of everyone whose face they ever reflected. Why else would it be bad luck to break a mirror? This particular mirror held the reflections of my parents when they were young and me as a child so it was my responsibility to keep it with me...forever. The look on her face told me there was, at least in her view, nothing normal about this belief and started me thinking that perhaps I was a bit odd.

Time went by, and I didn't give it much thought, until the day when a table spoke to me in an antique store. I was there to purchase a long coveted round, oak pedestal table for my dining room. Standing right next to my table of choice was a not round, not oak, not pedestal table that had apparently just arrived. Within earshot, the store owner was talking to one of his staff and relating the story of how the table had spent its life with an elderly man who had just gone into assisted living.

It's pretty beat up, he said, *but I didn't have the heart to tell him I didn't want it when he told me that his kids had done their homework on it, and his family ate dinner there every night.*

That did it for me. I left my dream table in the store and bought the one with the story. It was definitely used long and hard, but once I heard its background I needed to "save" it. From what I really don't know. Abandonment maybe, or worse yet the kindling pile. Refinished and restored, it stands in my dining room till this day, collecting *my* family stories of holiday dinners, grandchildrens' art projects and meals and laughter shared with friends over the years. Often when I sit at that table and write I feel in the company of the long ago children who once sat there before me. Its presence still brings me joy, but is also a daily reminder of something not quite right about my thought processes.

I am now at a place in my life where there is no denying my oddness. It plays out in innumerable situations often when I least expect it. When, for example, I cannot throw away the pieces of a colorful glass duckling that was mine as a child even though it has been tragically shattered beyond repair; when my heart breaks to see old houses demolished because I believe that bricks and mortar, lath and plaster hold our stories, and once they are gone so also are the stories they once held that no one is still alive to remember; when I always make sure to tuck in the stuffed animals along with my grandchildren as part of our bedtime ritual, being careful that their little noses as well as those of my grandchildren are not covered. The list is endless.

For many years I had a therapist with whom I freely shared my soul secrets. We discussed my dysfunctional parents, irrational fears, ill-fated marriage, free-floating anxiety, you name it, we discussed it all. Except, that is, my unusual identification with things inanimate. I believe I never brought it up because it spoke to a level of disconnection that I thought was so peculiar to me that he would not have any idea how to deal with it. Plus, there was a whole part of me that didn't think it necessary to be cured of this thinking. It was just a part of my unique perception of reality.

This misconception was proved wrong last week when my teenaged granddaughters, Margot and Elena, and I were out for an afternoon of lunch and shopping. At lunch, reminiscent of the girl talk I once loved, we discussed many things, dress codes in high school, boyfriends (theirs), sick friends (mine), their knowing every lyric to every song in *Hamilton* and all that they loved about the play. There was a momentary lull in the conversation, and then Margot broke the silence with, *Gigi, want to hear something weird?* Without waiting for my answer and with a little giggle she said, *Elena thinks stuffed animals have souls!*

Elena looked at me a bit (you should pardon the expression) sheepishly, and they both waited for my response. Without pausing for a second, I replied.

Me, too, Sweetheart, me, too.

I Don't Need a Genie

Fumiko Tokunaga Jensen

Someone once asked me what I would wish if a genie offered to change my appearance. When I was growing up in Japan, to be attractive you were supposed to have a pair of long legs, a short body, and white skin. A flat nose was a no-no. A pair of big eyes was a must.

I have four older sisters and the two oldest sisters were almost like mother figures to me because of the big age difference. The Number Three and Number Four Sisters were not good friends with each other. They were constantly quarreling, though when they wanted to tease me, they always teamed up. They used to tell me that I was found on the street. When I asked my mother if it was true, she said if they (my mother and father) had found a baby to bring home, they would have chosen a boy since they already had four girls. For me, this was a convincing answer.

My sisters often told me that my legs were too short, my body too long, my nose too flat, and my skin too dark to be beautiful. Fortunately,

I didn't suffer from those critiques. I guess I didn't care so much. I had accepted the truth that I was not very attractive.

When I was studying in Denmark, one day I went to a movie theater with several friends. There was not much leg space in front of the seats. Then one of them said, "It's OK for Fumiko, but it's so uncomfortable for us long-legged creatures." It wasn't meant to be a negative judgment of my short legs. Rather it was an envious statement. This was one of my "A-Ha" moments.

On another occasion, several people were competing about whose arms were the darkest after a summer vacation. When I held out my arm, too, they complained, saying, "This is not fair, Fumiko was born with darker skin to start with."

A Japanese proverb says that different places have different values. Thus I've learned the stereotypes from which my sisters teased me did not hold much value. Especially on airplanes, despite being teased about my short legs, I always feel so blessed being short-legged and feel sorry for long-legged people like my husband and my son. I feel good about being free from worrying about my looks and to accept what I was born with.

The last time I was in Japan, as I talked with my Number Four Sister, I realized she still got stuck in the same old stereotype idea. I tried to tell her the cautionary tale from my experiences but I doubt she understood it. I really wish she could be free from those meaningless thoughts about appearances, because I love her and wish her to be happy and confident with herself.

But alas, older sisters tend not to like to be lectured from younger sisters.

Who's Looking Anyway?

Trudi Goodman

Take note, I say to myself, of all the women out there with their upper arm flab gesturing hello and waving goodbye. I envy the ladies who are proud to dress in sleeveless tee shirts and blouses and are not afraid to show some skin, even lots of it, even unattractive skin. You're the courageous ones, I think, and it's apparent to me you just don't give a damn. Let it all hang out. Let the skin fall where it may. I'm so in awe!

Dangling loose wrinkled skin now appears on all parts of my body, but somehow the upper arm flab is more problematic for me, and I am a coward, although perhaps a misguided one. There is an entire group of us, a support system that says no matter what the season your upper arm flab needs to be fully covered and hidden from the naked eye. Alas the warm weather will arrive and again I will be faced with my UPPER ARM FLAB. To show or not to show, that is the question.

For probably the last thirty years of my existence, my bones (currently in trouble themselves with osteoporosis) have been supporting a slow-motion landslide of valuable epidermis. Now hear the truthful words of an aging female—my tush skin's connecting to my thigh skin, my thigh skin's connecting to my knee skin, my knee skin's connecting to my ankle skin, so bless my weary bones.

However, upper arm flab is my focus. I've been put in my place by women of various sizes, different shapes, and all ages. For instance, my younger sister has blurted out, "And is anyone noticing you anyway? No one cares about arms, especially yours." She adds, "As of late, they show a remarkable resemblance to Neapolitan ice cream. The hands and wrists are brown, the forearms pink, and your hidden upper arms milk white. Guess which parts haven't been touched by the light of day."

Why is she comfortable showing off her beautiful toasty brown skin that, by the way, is always sun-kissed because six months of the year she lives in Florida? Sister dearest is one of the fearless who are unafraid to sit by a pool surrounded by hundreds of eyes and wagging tongues wearing a skimpy, low-cut tank top. Can you be any braver? What's wrong with me, I wonder, we have the same parents.

When I was a little girl, I had my first encounter with upper arm flab. My mother's mother lived with us and was never shy about being who she was. Because of the hot summers in Chicago, Grandma—like any of the other normal women of her generation—would wear her sleeveless dresses. It was no big deal to show her aging imperfections. My sister and I would often play with her soft, milky white skin as though it were made of clay. Thoughtlessly, we would pull at the flab trying to make shapes. She would laugh along with her granddaughters, and many times said, "This will be you someday." And the stupid that can only be associated with the young would answer, "Oh no it won't. I won't let it." RIGHT!

Every spring, when the trees are budding, the tulips pushing through the ground, and the birds are chirping while feeding their newborn, I face my full-length mirror and give a wave to my upper arms and make plans with my best friend to find the latest in ladies' three-quarter-length sleeve arm attire.

"The dress designers have abandoned us. They couldn't care less about the aging," I mumble to my friend. She and I were appalled at the amount of tank tops piled high on the shelves of our store *du jour*. There seemed to be a complete lack of appropriate attire for the mature woman and her arms. The hours ticked by without any purchases being made in the six or seven stores we visited. I joked about all the merchandise that would be left for the merchants to deal with at the end of the season because we elders weren't buying into their choices. They'll be sorry when they have to ship the goods off to the discount stores. They never learn!

My friend and I decide to shop again soon. Closer to summer might be better. We hug and say our goodbyes, wrapping arms around each other in strong, firm holds. My friend goes home and will cook dinner for her husband. Her arms can carry dishes to the table and lift heavy pots and pans on the stove. I hate to grocery shop, but one needs to eat and the cupboard is bare, so I'm off to the nearest supermarket. I try not to buy too much. I live in a building without an elevator but with many steps. I'll walk up the several flights to my apartment, my arms schlepping the brown paper bags stuffed with the groceries. So I tell myself to get real. In the scheme of things, I had better focus on what arms are for.

Speaking Out

Tallis Wild

Susan E. Cohen

I enter your temple
Where it is rumored
That women wear tallises
There's one left lying crumpled
In the box by the door
And I wonder—
Dare I don it?
Is it true,
The tales that I've heard
That the women here actually put on
Those white fringed garments
Reserved for men only
These past three thousand years.

What if I take it
And it's the last one
And some man arrives
Who is supposed to wear a tallis
And I'm using it—

The last surviving tallis in this congregation
Where I am, after all, a newcomer.

And what if I take it and go in
And I'm the only woman wearing one, a pariah?
And what if I'd ever worn one
Back in my small New England congregation?
There would have been such an upheaval
Wearing a tallis inside my family synagogue
Would be the same as disrobing outside of it.

I put on the tallis
Wondering if it is accustomed to long, heavy hair.
Generations of women moan,
Wearers of all shawls but prayer shawls.
My ancestors stir in their burial garments.

The next day I bring my mother to the temple
I place one on her shoulders
And reluctantly, even fearfully, she accepts.
I am so pleased—my mother
Who in her time was strapped down to deliver a baby
Whereas I bore mine sitting upright
As if traveling on horseback.
She sat as a girl in a synagogue
With the men and women planted in separate pews.

Suddenly I go tallis wild

I am filled with mad urges.

I want to place a tallis on my dead grandmother

Who newly arrived, sewed in a sweatshop

And made blouses, skirts, dresses

But never a tallis

And if she'd woven one

Could not have worn it anyway.

A tender of geese, cows, children

She still made it her business

To be one of the first in line

When color movies came to town.

She would not have minded

A new wearing of an ancient garment.

I need old tallises

Hundreds, thousands of them

To cover the shorn heads

Of the women of Auschwitz

And I need to weave new ones

For all my disenchanted sisters

Who are Jews but won't be

Because it's a sexist religion.

And, while we're at it,

How about an interfaith tallis

For the nun who spoke up to the Pope?

And a tallis for my mother-in-law

Who supposedly doesn't believe

And spends hours and hours

Making chicken soup for each holiday
And wears white on Yom Kippur
In spite of herself.

I need for myself
A very large tallis to hide under
So I could really pray.
A tallis to cry beneath next to my husband
A tallis to shuckle back and forth under
A tallis to both chant in and shriek
A tallis within which I wrap myself and dance.
What better place for a tallis
Than draped over my milk-filled breasts?

And lastly, just two more tallises—
One for my nine-week-old son
Who looking down from the heavens for centuries
Was born expecting it,
And one to put aside
For my as yet unconceived daughter
For whom it may come as a surprise.

The Sinner

Marie Davidson

Calvin was a small, slight man in his late twenties. He had protruding front teeth and a wispy goatee. He was neatly dressed in a blue sweat suit, running shoes, and a Chicago Cubs baseball cap that was way too big for his head. Calvin arrived for his first appointment at the mental health clinic accompanied by his mother and stepfather. From the doorway to the waiting room, I noticed he was rocking back and forth in his chair. He looked scared.

I knew from the clinic intake report that Calvin had been diagnosed in early childhood as "mildly retarded," although the current term in use was "developmentally disabled." He was functioning at about the level of a ten-year-old. The supervisor at Calvin's job had referred the family to my clinic, which exclusively served adults with mental and emotional disabilities. Calvin's behavior at work had changed recently and he was having emotional outbursts and scaring his co-workers. He was also writing notes that said "Calvin get hurt," "Calvin get punish," and "hell."

When Calvin saw me enter the waiting room, he stood up and extended a shaking hand. Fixing me with his deep brown eyes, he said, "Hi. I'm Calvin. Who are you going to be?"

I took his hand. "Hi, Calvin. My name is Marie and I'm going to be your therapist, which means I want to help you feel better. " Calvin put his face a few inches from mine and asked, "How are you going to do that?"

Honestly, I had no idea. I was a brand-new therapist working in a relatively new clinic. In 1982 there were very few mental health services available for people with developmental disabilities.

In our first few sessions, I found out a lot about Calvin. As Calvin became more comfortable with me, he seemed to enjoy my attention. I learned about his life at home with his family and how he put together first-aid kits at his job. Calvin told me he was a Catholic and his family attended Our Lady of Perpetual Sorrows church every week on the South Side of Chicago. He was also an ardent Cubs fan, and a walking encyclopedia of Cubs' history and the latest developments at Wrigley Field. The Cubs were entrenched in the longest slump in baseball history. "I don't know why they don't win more," Calvin said with a catch in his voice. "They haven't made the playoffs since 1945."

Calvin was a big worrier. He told me he was scared a lot, and his biggest fears were about being punished and going to hell. Calvin had spent several years in a Catholic residential school as an adolescent, where he had absorbed a lot of teachings about sin, including the idea that even thoughts could be sins. Calvin was convinced he was being punished and he didn't know what he had done wrong.

"I'm going to hell. I must have sinned. It's why I'm a retard. The Cubs, maybe they sinned, and have that curse so they can't win games. I hope the Cubs won't go to hell, too."

I visited Calvin at his workplace, where his co-workers were all developmentally disabled. He was thrilled. He beamed and bounced up and down, telling his co-workers, "That's her, that's my therapist, that lady, she talks nice to me and she's a Cubs fan, too." Paul, the supervisor at the workshop, told me that Calvin had started his odd behavior after his best friend at the workshop, Diana, left when her family moved to Texas. Paul thought Calvin missed his friend and maybe had the idea that losing the friend was punishment for something he'd done. Calvin's recent outbursts in the workshop were putting his job in jeopardy.

The director at my mental health clinic thought Calvin had a psychotic condition and needed coaching in how to manage his delusions and inappropriate outbursts. I agreed about the coaching, but thought the top priority was to help Calvin free himself of his fears of eternal damnation and accept himself as a good human being who was not a sinner. As a former Catholic, I was only too familiar with the scary parts of Catholic doctrine. Although Calvin had been baptized and went to church with his family, he had never had the experience of making a confession and being forgiven by a priest. My goal for Calvin was to get him to a priest who would hear his confession and absolve him of sins, real or imaginary.

The Cubs would just have to take care of themselves.

I got in touch with the Pastor at Our Lady of Perpetual Sorrows, Father Brown. He agreed to meet Calvin and see what he could do. I told Calvin's parents about the plan and they were surprised but agreeable. We set a date six weeks later for Calvin to meet Father Brown.

In the meantime, Calvin and I worked on preparing him for his first confession and also on what we called "God questions." Calvin said, "I want you to help me write my prayers. And I want to do the holy sacraments with you." I was impressed with the depth of Calvin's religious concerns. I worried if I would be up to this task.

The irony was that I was working with Calvin in a religious tradition I had rejected. Because he asked me, I had told Calvin I was raised Catholic. I had been taught from the Baltimore Catechism, just as he had been. What I didn't share was that I had left the church years ago. It was a painful subject.

I had long nursed a grudge about the secondary position of women in the church and particularly how they were not allowed to be priests. Now I was going to step up to the plate for Calvin, minister to his spiritual needs, and help him work through his Catholic God questions. I checked in with the clinic director, a secular Jewish atheist. He thought it was a mad but creative treatment plan. "Let's see what happens. Is this to help Calvin or is it for you, too?" A good question. I thought it might be for both of us.

Each of our sessions for the next few weeks began with Calvin dictating a prayer. I would read it back to him and we would conclude with a fervent "Amen." The prayers were all similar.

"Dear God, this is Calvin talking to you, please listen to me. Thank you for the good things I have. Thank you for my running shoes and my Cubs jacket. I have two questions. First, why haven't the Cubs won the World Series since 1908? They play so hard—they should win. And, why aren't I normal? I know I've sinned but I don't know what I did. I am trying my best. Please God, make me normal."

We also began to role-play sacraments. We did Baptism first. I poured pretend Holy Water on Calvin's forehead and asked him if he renounced Satan and all his works. "Yes!" Calvin shouted. "Then I baptize you Calvin, in the name of the Father, the Son, and the Holy Ghost." Calvin burst out in delighted laughter. "This is my new good beginning!"

We moved on to Holy Communion, receiving the body of Christ in the form of a specially consecrated bread wafer. I was a bit spooked to be role-playing this with Calvin, even though I no longer believed in transubstantiation, when the bread becomes Christ's body through the power of the priest and his words. I considered using a Necco Wafer candy—the cinnamon white one—but I went with a Ritz cracker instead. It was flat, bread-like, and tasty. I took a Ritz in my hands and lifted it up. "*Hoc est enim corpus meum.* This is my body." Calvin was awed. "You know Latin." He looked at me with new appreciation. I had to admit that this was my childhood dream of being a priest come true for me. I smiled at Calvin with what I hoped was a benevolent priestess-like visage.

The next sacrament on our list was Penance, the confession of sins. I talked to Father Brown on the phone again, explaining Calvin's distress and how certain teachings had led him to think he was a terrible sinner. I emphasized how important I thought it was for Calvin's spiritual health to have a proper confession. Father Brown said he would hear Calvin's confession in his study at the rectory. The priest gave me his word that he would absolve Calvin.

For two weeks Calvin and I practiced going to confession. Calvin would say, "Bless me, father, for I have sinned. This is my first confession." I told him his sins were private and he would only tell them to the priest.

The appointed day for meeting Father Brown at Our lady of Perpetual Sorrows came and Calvin's mother took him to the church rectory. In the afternoon my phone rang. It was Calvin's mother.

"Father wouldn't hear Calvin's confession, Dr. Marie. He told me afterwards that Calvin wasn't sophisticated enough to have a valid confession. They did talk for a while about something but it surely didn't work out for Calvin the way we hoped. Calvin is devastated."

A spark of rage kindled in my gut. I could imagine Calvin and the priest in the rectory study, the self-important pompous cleric taking one look at Calvin and seeing only a funny-looking, mentally handicapped guy in a mis-sized Cubs hat. He thought Calvin was too dumb to receive the sacrament of penance. Father Brown had no idea that he was in the presence of a thoughtful theologian looking for comfort from his church.

At our next session, Calvin walked slowly to our therapy room, looking glum. "Father didn't hear my confession. He didn't forgive me. I told him about how I wasn't normal and that my mom is sad sometimes. And about the Cubs and way they are cursed. I asked why God did these things. Father didn't listen to me, not like you do. He talked on the phone and looked at stuff on his desk. I think he's maybe for the White Sox, too."

"I am really sorry, Calvin. Father Brown should have heard your confession. I guess even priests make mistakes."

"Father said I have to accept the way I am. He said that God always answers our prayers, but not always the way we want Him to."

I silently agreed with Father Brown on those points, at that moment conceding I was not a true atheist. But not hearing Calvin's confession was a mortal sin, in my opinion, and Father Brown was going to hell.

"Calvin," I asked, "Would you like to be absolved of your sins?"

"Yes."

I made a leap of faith. If I could transubstantiate a Ritz cracker, why couldn't I absolve sins?

There was no confessional screen to separate me from Calvin. I was not ordained as a priest, but I was trained in the care of souls. I knew I could forgive Calvin for all the sins he never committed and help him to stop fearing hell and look forward to eternal salvation instead. The confidentiality of the confessional and of the therapy room do not allow me to divulge what Calvin confessed, but it was striking how much his "sins" had to do with when he failed to be kind to others and how he might somehow be influencing the Cubs' lack of post-season play. His penitential fears boiled down to "What if God decides I'm not good enough to go to heaven? And what if he's not a Cubs' fan?"

"Calvin, *ego absolvo te a peccatis tuis in nomine patris, et filii, et spiritus sancti.* I absolve you of your sins in the name of the Father, and of the Son, and of the Holy Ghost."

He was absolved. He was developmentally disabled. He was a Cubs fan. He was Calvin. I loved him enormously. I made a slow, sweeping sign of the cross with my right arm and said, "For your penance, you have to write a new prayer. Let's get to work."

"Ok!" Calvin said, giving me a huge smile.

It Happened One Night

Anne Haack Sullivan

When she thinks about their encounter that Friday night, there are only a few things she remembers distinctly. Following him into a shadowed bedroom. The gray light of a nearby streetlamp filtering through a thin, drawn shade. A brief flash of pain. And the demanding touch of his full pink lips.

The next Monday at school, whispers ricocheted off the metal lockers. *Easy. Whore. Slut.* In U.S. History class a friend took her aside to repeat the rumors, her eyes betraying subtle disapproval. In the girl's bathroom, a conversation overheard. *Did you hear she did it with him at the party? Who knew she was like that?* That afternoon she confronted him near a drinking fountain, summoning a reservoir of courage she hadn't known she possessed. Her face burned with rage and shame. Why had he spread a rumor that simply wasn't true? A shrug of his shoulders. A smirk. The way he looked over her shoulder as she spoke, never making eye contact. No apology. No admission of guilt.

Next period, as the Advanced Chem teacher stood before an overhead projector droning about equilibrium, she tried to recreate the night in her head. Entering the nondescript ranch-style house. Laughing at the host wearing a toga. The beat of the music reverberating through the floor. Angling the beer keg spigot against the rim of a plastic cup to minimize foam. There might have been a quarters game. Maybe a vodka shot. Maybe several. It was just like any other party. Any normal Friday night. Except for him. His presence above her in the murky darkness. And waking up the next morning at home not knowing how she got there.

Before that night, she'd been the kind of girl you can't quite place at the twentieth reunion. Acceptable, not pretty. Smart, not gifted. Neither popular nor a misfit. A girl destined to drift through high school without anyone really noticing. But not the boy. He worked hard to draw attention. Filling up all the space in a room with his derisive laugh. Harrassing stoop-shouldered frizzy-haired girls with his jock gang outside the cafeteria. They guarded their turf in matching team windbreakers and indoor soccer shoes, jeering at the acne-faced freshmen boys who were still praying each night for puberty. Without his yellow coat and obnoxious friends, he, too, might have been just another face in the yearbook. Neither handsome nor plain. Mousy brown hair worn in a feathered shag. Glinting braces and watery blue eyes, his features neither ugly nor striking. Except for the outsized pink lips that had hovered over her face.

After their confrontation he never again acknowledged her. In less than a week, the talk died down. The people who mattered to themselves found someone else to gossip about and other rumors to start. They were no longer interested in her or what might have happened on a beer-infused night at a random house party. The boy and his friends went on as before. There were Shakespeare soliloquies to memorize and term papers to write.

Football games to attend and student council candy to sell. But nothing was the same for her. She felt vulnerable and exposed passing through the hallways, haunted by the cruel rumors and the fear they could start again.

She told herself it was her own fault. She drank too much that night. She followed him willingly down that hallway. He didn't drag her. She didn't really know what happened beyond the bedroom door. The barely recognizable flashes felt more like imagination than memory. Was there a quilt? An oak headboard? The picture had been ripped into incongruent pieces by the hand of alcohol, haphazardly taped together, and missing the parts necessary to make a congruent image. No matter how many nights she stayed awake thinking, there wasn't any more she could remember. Eventually she shoved her shameful mistake way down into her soul and buried it, like a piece of garbage at the bottom of an overfilled bin, forcing the hurt and confusion to sink from the surface of her consciousness. That night. That boy. Floating somewhere in the deepest part of her mind's ocean. Dark. Hidden. Inaccessible.

Until thirty years later, a magazine story about college rape culture raised hairs on the back of her neck. Her heart accelerated, cheeks flaming with forgotten humiliation. The wound was still open, merely bandaged by time, not healed. And with the remembered pain, a new thought. One she'd been too shocked and hurt to consider all those decades ago. Maybe the boy hadn't lied about that night, just about her willing participation. Along with whole pieces of the evening's memories, did drinking also steal her ability to give consent?

The man who was once that boy wouldn't remember. He wouldn't know her if they passed on the street today. But she'd know him anywhere. His high cheekbones. The deeply set eyes, spaced just a little too far apart. The arrogant tilt of his jaw. And the lips she remembered on her neck and shoulders, pressing her hard into pillows that may have been paisley or flowered. The lips that had remained mutely closed when she confronted him. The lips that didn't move in her defense. The lips that would never admit to a crime.

The truth of that night would forever remain a feeling, never a fact. Her memories were lost, unable to confirm or refute her dark suspicions. But some things were undeniable. He took advantage. He spread the rumors. He was the shameful one. She could free herself from the guilt and self-recrimination. She could be angry, not sad or humiliated.

Whatever happened that night, she could be certain. She was not to blame.

Kung Pow

Catherine Davis

I sit across the table from you,
The Chinese food in front of us
Cooling rapidly.

You have not stopped talking since we sat down:

Your foodie blog and
Your friend from high school who has personal problems and
The boyfriend you followed to California in the eighties and
The therapist you take your kid to and

and

I nod my head, looking at congealing Kung Pao Shrimp,
Wondering what happened to the time

When we used to joke and laugh,
Compare notes about motherhood,
Fashion tips, and where to buy the best

Shoes

I was so grateful for you, telling myself this was what it must be like,
Convincing myself we were best friends.
Now you suck on your second Mai Tai
And just keep talking.

Our dinner has grown cold.

I offer to pay the bill, a gesture of regret
and remorse

And as we get up to leave, I think
Goodbye. And good riddance.

I will not be taking home the leftovers, thank you

Coming Out of the Closet

Susan E. Cohen

I do a pretty good job of passing for normal. I almost always wear gym shoes so people assume I'm some sort of athlete who jogs at dawn or is about to pop onto the nearest treadmill. I actually wear them because, besides being comfortable and supportive and a little more bouncy than a traditional shoe, they save tiny shreds of energy. I usually leave my purse in the car—my keys in one pocket and my phone in the other saves carrying weight—more precious shards of energy. When I travel with my husband, he will bravely carry my purse for me at times to save my strength. If I am feeling well enough, I take it back from him. I always do as much as I can—he understands that; he knew who I was before I got sick. He is really the only person still alive who has fully witnessed my struggle behind the scenes.

I sit wherever I can—cocktail parties are the worst. People like to stand at parties in America—that way if a few minutes of chitchat is not highly rewarding, you can effortlessly move on to someone else. I know, because I sit at cocktail parties and wait for the courageous soul who will come and take the risk of committing to sit down next to someone. I have been known to sit and even have to lay down sometimes in very unusual places, the floors of airports, the floors of supermarkets; anywhere you end up standing in line, you may find me sitting, which is why I usually wear pants.

I have an illness for which there is no cure nor any real treatments, a disease that does not sound like a disease, but is more disabling than most. When I am really ill, no one sees me except my family. You can only find me horizontal, laying on our bed or, if I am too weak to make it upstairs, laying on the couch; in either case my legs angled up against the wall at first to let the pooled blood circulate back. I will lay there for hours feeling like I am cloaked in death, a toxic sensation completely taking over that renders me helplessly weak and powerless to move, the body's very effective way of telling you that you have overstepped your limits. At that point you don't get to decide whether you can do more or not. The body cannot go further. Pain in the lymph nodes, lots and lots of pain. This is another feature that people don't seem to grasp. No matter if I have tried to explain the illness before (which is why I usually don't bother), any time I mention pain, folks invariably comment, "I never realized you have pain." Most of the time, because I do not complain and am out of sight when I am severely ill, they do not even realize or remember that I am not well.

Contrary to popular opinion, stress does not make me ill—only using physical energy will do that. Walking too long (and "too long" is not very long indeed), whether on a beach or a garden path or just on the street where I live, will render me hopelessly sick. A short spurt of dancing, my formerly most favorite of all human pursuits, will make me ill very quickly.

Carrying, lifting, hiking, biking, cross-county skiing, tennis—all out of the question. "Face it," I was told at a medical conference by an exercise physiologist, "Your aerobic system is broken." I am forced to live like an invalid, while my body yearns to play like an athlete. I cook in the kitchen sitting on a high chair. I make brief "healthy" appearances and then I lay down.

I am a whole lot better than I used to be. For the first five years of the illness, I was bedridden much of the time. I could make it to the bathroom and the table to eat, but not a whole lot more. By experiencing overwhelming weakness, I am now able to understand how people actually die even when they desperately want to live more than anything else. I constantly come to terms with the limits of willpower, something that our culture does not accept. We battle our diseases in America, we fight the good fight, we overcome, except when we can't. Until I had this illness, I did not understand how the mind, no matter how strong its willpower, must eventually bow to the body. With this disease, I learn this lesson over and over again.

And yet . . . every time I start to feel even a trifle better for part of a day, my optimistic side takes over and starts to seduce myself. Maybe I am improving, maybe I can walk a little further, maybe I can keep going. It is hard to believe that someone can keep fooling themselves over and over like a built-in Charlie Brown, but that is exactly how I live. One doctor called me "the ultimate masker." What I really am is a consummate amateur actress, playing the role of a healthy person for the public, playing the role of a not-so-sick person for my physicians, my acquaintances and, ultimately, for myself.

Which is why people occasionally still invite me to travel with them. I am an adventurer at heart, but these good meaning people have no idea of how I would hold them back. I can't go to the marketplace in the early morning and then through the museum and then on to the palace, the temple, the ruins. Only in my fantasies. I imagine that if I am in a different, exotic country, I will inhabit a different body, my real body, the body I was born with, the body that had limitless energy the first 24 years of my life, the real me.

Obviously, I still have not integrated the sick person I am with my self-concept. In my heart, I aspire to be an adventurer. In my brain, I am a popcorn popper of plans and temptations. In reality, I can do one activity and, on a good day, maybe two, but not day-after-day in a row. On a bad day I have to be still. I have to wait for the temporary reprieve that recovery mode will eventually bring. Have I ever been well for a whole week in the last four decades? I would have to say no. How about a few days in a row? You mean, the whole day, all of those few days? No. One whole day? In the first thirty years, never. Now, once in a great while, it happens. This is an illness that never leaves you. It inhabits you, it stands ready to consume you, it shadows you in the rare moments you appear to live normal.

Do I describe this to you now because I seek pity or sympathy—unequivocally, no. I describe it only so you have a chance of understanding how I live, that I inhabit a completely different world, that I function in a very unstable universe of illness, where things change every few hours and, therefore, for which I must make constant accommodations. That to my consternation, I find myself a delicate flower who cannot abide the cold, who can get a sore throat followed by bronchitis from a brief chill. I am someone who once canoed down the Allagash River, who camped outside in the winter, who worked as one of the first female mailmen—a person who ran along the beach for the sheer joy of movement. I remember myself going out to dance in the rain…

When I first became ill, I was diagnosed with leukemia, then Hodgkin's disease, then "nothing" because the disease I suffered from had not been named or even discovered yet. Our physicians knew they could not cure everything, but they thought they could, at least, render a diagnosis. If your complaints did not fit into one of the medical sorting boxes, you simply could not be ill. "You must have more symptoms," I was told. "You must have fewer." "You should get married," the infectious disease specialist counseled. "You should work on your brilliant doctoral dissertation," the Mayo Clinic advised. I was told time and time again, "If you were a man, this would not bother you," and, "If you got married, this would probably all go away."

The disease I have was originally called CFS for "Chronic Fatigue Syndrome," in this country, then briefly referred to as CFIDS for "Chronic Fatigue Immune Deficiency Syndrome." There was a quick flirtation with "Neuroendrocrine Immune Disorder," while Myalgic Encephalomyelitis or ME has been the title for a long time in most other countries. At the moment the medical choice of our national experts is a combo platter name of ME/CFS. The reference to "chronic fatigue" makes the illness sound like people are tired. Let's face it, everyone in America is tired. Tired is nothing. We have all been tired. Tired is something you push through. You have a cup of coffee, you shake yourself out of it, you soldier on. Tired is not Chronic Fatigue Syndrome. Profound debilitating weakness—now that is ME/CFS.

A new Institute of Medicine committee, supposedly validating the illness as a real disease, just recently proposed "SEID" for "Systemic Exertional Intolerance Disease," which unfortunately conjures up the image of a "couch potato" or perhaps aged people propped up in wheel chairs in the halls of a nursing home.

Last weekend I attempted a brief walk in the Botanic Garden with a good friend. "Are you sure this isn't too much for you?" she, who knows me well, asked. "No, I love it," I answered bravely. "The fresh air feels so good, the walking really lifts my spirits." By the time she dropped me off at my car, I was beginning the descent. This phenomenon—a severe reaction to even relatively mild physical exertion—is a hallmark of the illness called Post Exertional Malaise or PEM. I barely managed to drive home and get into the house as I felt the illness gathering momentum and then completely taking over. I cancelled our Saturday night plans; I stayed home Sunday waiting for the siege to pass. I was still in pain and enveloped with weakness at bedtime.

I had a lot of time to think. I thought about how nobody, except those who are stricken or their close family members who live with them on a daily basis, really understands this illness. I thought about how I hide it most of the time. And, as I lay there, feeling like I was dying, I decided that perhaps it was time to come out of the closet.

Sleight of Hand

Ruth Sterlin

I was eager to start junior high. Sock hops, class rings, and a different teacher for every subject! It was going to be an adventure compared to watching my sixth-grade teacher smile across her prominent two front teeth as she spirited nouns and verbs across the chalkboard in her passion for diagramming sentences.

In spite of my boredom in sixth grade, I actually liked my teacher, Mrs. East. After school, I used to hang around outside her classroom knowing that eventually she would invite me back in to help her with clean up. She was so easy to talk to and seemed to sense that I was in no rush to get home. At home, I knew that my mother would be deeply engrossed in her meticulous housework, my father would be at work, and Mr. Popularity in the form of my older brother would still be at high school where he had all but set up residence.

My brother would show up just in time for dinner, however. This was the one time each day when we were all together. Unfortunately, the hot steaming food was generally accompanied by harsh-sounding political debates between my brother and my father—my sister would join in if she was home from college. I couldn't quite figure out if these argumentative exchanges were actually about politics or about something else altogether, since my father and brother always ended up angry with each other. My mother avoided these dark undertones by serving us our food or clearing the table. I would try to creep up to my room, before my parents began their own postprandial arguments.

Somehow June found its way onto the calendar, and on the last day of school, I slipped a card on to Mrs. East's desk. This time, after the final bell, I turned to her at the door and waved goodbye. Standing in front of her desk, she held up my card and waved back. When I saw her take a step towards me, I hurried down the hall, not wanting to feel my sadness. I told myself that I would be happier in junior high.

Junior high had definite shock value, given the unexpected sound of yelling, laughter and lockers slamming, after six years of being shushed in school hallways. The boys seemed surprisingly taller, and, like me, a lot of the girls were filling out their sweaters. It made my insides tingle.

Over the summer, I'd discovered a box of clothing in our utility room at home. As I rummaged through it, I couldn't believe what was hiding there. *Bras!* I waited until my mother went out before carrying one of them into the bathroom to try it on. After adjusting the straps, I looked into the bathroom mirror. Oh, my God, it fit! I quickly tried on the rest of the bras, one by one, trying to finish before my mother came home.

It took me a whole week to work up the courage to tell my mother about the bras. When I finally showed them to her, she laughed, saying that she had forgotten they were even there. Something about her laughter bothered me. Bras were a very serious matter. My friends were already telling me, "You know, Ruth, you need a bra!" How could she have forgotten something so important?

When I think back to junior high, it seemed to be all about boys, bras, and Kotex pads. I remember my friends and me talking about all of it, whispering in corners with red cheeks. Reaching puberty made me vacillate between tremendous excitement and a sense of overwhelm, as if I were mounting a steep spiral staircase with no hand rails to guide me. Who was this person I was becoming? Did other people notice the changes in me?

One morning I found out that it was all showing. I was in bed when I heard my father answer the phone in the hallway. I could tell by the conversation that he was talking to my grandmother.

"Guess what?" I heard him say loudly. "Ruth Ann is wearing *brassieres* now!" Oh God. I pulled the blankets over my head. Didn't he know that my bras were private. What an idiot he was to announce it to the whole world!

At school, the hallways were full of hormones, whizzing by faster than a speeding bullet. The tumult of swishing skirts, slamming lockers, and unwelcome pimples made it impossible to sort out whose hormones were whose. By the middle of the year, I noticed that teachers had them, too.

Noticeably, the seventh-grade language arts teacher all the girls had a crush on, Mr. Johnson, who chaperoned our school dances. He had a charisma that made us all laugh at his jokes and vie for his approval. A number of times during class he teased me about my fluffy red-brown hair and my laugh. At one of the dances he even came over and said he'd like to dance with me. I saw this as just another one of his jokes, although I'd come to look forward to his increasing attention.

Then came Will. He had a sweet smile and Howdy-Doody cheeks, which were usually flushed when he looked for me before class. We made eyes at each other across the aisle of the bus on school field trips and sometimes even held hands. Of course, we were too frightened to touch any of the body parts we learned about in health class. *This is what it's like to have a boyfriend,* I thought!

Nonetheless, I spent a lot of time after school in the language arts room finishing projects that Mr. Johnson had assigned. Will and I had drifted apart, and being in the language arts room reminded me of the comfort I used to feel with Mrs. East. Mr. Johnson would compliment me on my school work, sometimes even on my clothes. There was something about him that I found magical. He was like a magician who bedazzles his audience while pulling a rabbit out of his empty hat. How naive I was!

One day after school, Mr. Johnson sought me out in the hallway and told me to come into his classroom. He wanted to talk to me about something. The serious look on his face told me that it had to be important. Without hesitation, I came in his room, and he closed the door. He walked over to me until he was about a foot in front of me.

"I think there are some things you should know about boys," he said. I had no idea what he was talking about, but I was sure he would explain it to me.

"Here, let me show you." Mr. Johnson then proceeded to run his hands slowly over my breasts and then my buttocks. I was completed confused.

"This is how boys will secretly cop a feel," he said with his breath rising. "You need to watch out for them, especially when they dance with you." Dumbstruck, I stood paralyzed.

He then took a dance position with me and expertly brought his knee up between my legs and rubbed it around. I looked into his face, which looked strange and flushed, trying to understand what he was telling me, what he was doing. *Is he trying to protect me,* I asked myself? Is this okay? I realized that I had stopped breathing. Suddenly afraid, I pulled away and walked to the door.

"You shouldn't tell anyone about this," he said. "They won't understand."

I stumbled through the hallway, bypassing my locker, and went home feeling sick to my stomach. That night, I skipped dinner and headed straight upstairs to bed. My father must have been concerned, because he came up to check on me. I pretended to be asleep.

When human fingers brush the wing of a newly hatched butterfly, it will still be able to fly, just not as high. I continued to travel through my school days, doing my schoolwork and smiling at all my friends. In my discovery of the dark side of young sexuality—that it can easily become a target—I also discovered that I could hide behind my smile. I kept up a cheerful façade, surrounded by friends who truly seemed to like me, and hid from the whole episode. I avoided Mr. Johnson and found myself pretending that it had never even happened. It was the beginning of a long period in my life of splitting off my feelings from the rest of my inner self.

Years later, when I could finally talk about the incident with a trusted friend, I understood the impact of Mr. Johnson's cruelty. He was a magician indeed. He had bedazzled me while using his best sleight of hand to explore the tender places of my new womanhood. And the fact that he knew I wouldn't go home and tell my parents? Well, that was the most amazing trick of all.

I grieve for that young, smiling junior high girl who suddenly felt like damaged goods. Who believed that it was all her own fault. But even a damaged wing can't stop a butterfly from soaring.

A Death in the Family

Anne Haack Sullivan

This summer our neighborhood lost one of its oldest citizens. They said he was diseased and rotten inside, but you wouldn't know it. Despite old age, he'd served our community dutifully year after year, never resigning his responsibilities. Taller than a house, his limbs shielded decades of bikers and dog walkers and little boys being pulled to the beach in wagons. In bitter Januaries he gave stick arms for generations of snowmen.

He was already majestic when our town became a dot on the map. He'd stood half a century when the first trowels of stucco were applied to our home. Over the years, while the house passed from family to family, he was a constant. He welcomed new babies, helped say goodbye to cherished pets and watched children chase lightning bugs. When he was young, horse-drawn carriages wheeled by over bricks and under gas lamps. The lamps became streetlights, the bricks were paved over, but he remained in his corner of the yard waving branches at trick-or-treaters and neighbors sharing cocktails on the porch.

The bad news came in an official-looking envelope. The title beneath an illegible, computer-generated signature read "Village Arborist." A perfunctory paragraph told us our tree was a public hazard to be cut down on an unspecified summer day. Later that week, a tiny silver tag and hastily applied stripe of white paint announced his fate to passers by. But the tree didn't know.

In late spring he sprouted leaves, as he had for the last century. He wasn't infested with ash borers or stricken by Dutch Elm disease like the other trees being knocked down around town. He had no curdled leaves or lesions of torn, missing bark. Though I lacked any facility for gardening and hadn't been near a botany book since high school, I felt qualified to render an opinion on his health.

"That tree is not sick," I announced when my husband joined me beneath his trunk, craning his neck to see what I was pointing toward. "Where are the dead branches?"

He nodded in that way that husbands do and shrugged, answerless. He'd grown tired of what had already been several days of ranting. He wouldn't be joining me, I knew, if I strapped myself to the tree in protest.

Summer arrived and the last day of school came and went. Soon I'd awaken to whining saws and a shrieking wood chipper. I sat on my porch swing at night, wondering if tomorrow would be the day the tree would live no more. But the weeks blended into months and soon it was August. Growing weary of waiting, I pestered the arborist for a specific date. "Some time this month," was all the poor man could promise.

And then one Friday, without fanfare, the heavy equipment trucks rolled up. Safety cones were erected, blocking westbound traffic. Hard-hatted men in wraparound sunglasses anchored themselves a hundred feet up, yelling instructions to colleagues on the ground. They'd work their way down, hacking off branches. I thought of staying home to watch, but it was too painful. I looked out the front window to say goodbye and saw that the upper branches were already gone. The tree looked small and sad, a forlorn naked trunk waiting for decimation.

When I returned that evening only a stump was left. I stood on what was left of a 150-year life. I thought about *The Giving Tree*, a book I'd once read over and over to a freshly bathed boy and girl in footie pajamas. Our tree didn't give up his fruit or offer his trunk for a boat, but he'd given unconditionally to generations of neighborhood children. Colorful leaf piles to jump in. A home base for tag or hide-and-go-seek. A sturdy spot for a rope swing. Simple joys. Childhood memories.

Rest in peace, tree.

Revelations

Amherst, Late March

(with a nod to *Because I could not stop for Death*)

Catherine Davis

I kindly stopped for Emily Dickinson
In her house upon the hill.

From her bedroom window I searched for carriages that used to promenade
Expecting to hear the clop-clop of hooves
Only to hear trucks and cars
Rattle the rippled windowpanes as they passed.

And across the street, where there should have been
Fields of beans and corn, just sprouting in the spring rain
There were only dilapidated houses and telephone lines.

Stood in the once-spendid parlour
In her brother's house across the way,
Now an ancient pile of grandeur
Slowly moldering into nothing.

Disappointed, I turned away.

But then, for a moment:

I saw spring fields. Carriages promenading past.

The flick of a skirt past a fire in the fireplace.

Felt a little—heat?

Heard a little—laugh?

Then it all disappeared in a flash

And I found myself standing outside

On the cold concrete sidewalk in the cold March wind.

I kindly stopped for Emily Dickinson.

Or did she kindly stop for me?

Rite of Passage

Judy SooHoo

The number four is considered bad luck in Chinese culture. It sounds like the shrill word death (*schlé*) that declares itself from the poor cursed, flat monotone, number four (*schlé*). For more than a month, my eyes would catch the flashing of the red or black digital clock faces that read 4:44 with a frequency I had not seen before—early morning as well as afternoon. I don't consider myself superstitious but this unnerved me.

Our household included my son, my mother and me. Over seven years, we had four tragic deaths in the family, including that of my husband. I quickly set aside the possibility that my son or mother could be struck down as the others had. Instead, it was easier for me to focus on something I thought I could be in control of—our upcoming 17-hour road trip to Florida.

The vacation was trumpeted as our "last hurrah" before my son headed off to college. Although he chose a local university, I knew this was the beginning of the end of my parenting relationship as I had known it. Our connection had taken us through the summer to concerts and an art exhibit, because in "going with me he could take his time instead of rushing through, as he would have to with a friend." The relationship had certainly been tested during the teen years, but the realization didn't hit me until then that my days of guiding him rather than battling or molding him were over.

I enjoyed being the planner, navigator, and principal driver in our family and had logged thousands of miles over the years from jam-packed New York City, beautiful-but-dangerous US Route 1, to the treacherous Harz Mountains in Germany. Our 100-mile round trip commutes every weekend for seven years from Chicago to the western suburbs for my son's music and karate lessons, added to the running total. But gone were the days of carefree driving. My mind would wander passing intended stops, or I would nod off at the wheel during the unbroken hours-long stretches of road.

Fortunately, our trip down to Florida was fine, having heeded caution. We paid homage to the quirky roadside discoveries made over the years and recalled even more. Billboards of Kentucky Fried Chicken Buffets, Dinosaur World, Lion's Den Adult Stores and "Clean Bathrooms with Showers" that introduced us to the mysterious world of truckers queued up for their turns at second-floor showers.

The super-Walmarts of travel stores were a paradise for gadget and accessory freaks like me, and souvenir-lovers and bargain-seekers like my mother. Walls were lined with the biggest variety of drinks and snacks you could imagine. "Any-sized, 99¢ sodas"—120 ounces that required its own rest stop—teetering top-heavy and precariously in our cup holders. "Any-sized, Any flavor $1.69 Cappuccinos" steaming hot keeping us awake. And my favorite—the carousels of soulful, quaint, ever-appropriate, Blue Mountain Arts greeting cards of richly textured papers, touching poetry, and beautiful calligraphy and script.

The first week we were room-bound as my son completed his online college registration. During the second week, a hurricane made its way across the state closing down the resort's outdoor activities. When activities resumed, we took to the rock wall and zipline. I was cruelly misled as to how much difference a few years and a few pounds would make as I struggled to reach the top. While I was unsuccessful in my attempts, my son scrambled up all seven sides of the column. Ziplining for the first time went much better for me, simply stepping off the platform spurred on by my dismal showing on the rock wall.

The lake was now the remaining challenge. Unlike my son, I wasn't much of a swimmer. He knew nothing of my trepidation around water and had decided on jet skiing. We read the fine print: It required a driver's license. This meant that my son who had just received his driver's permit would have to ride with me.

I did a quick online search. There were the typical YouTube videos of novice jet skiers showing off their quick-found abilities. A safety video that demonstrated how to right an overturned jet ski did nothing to assuage my growing fears. I had no idea I had to balance this mechanical beast that could ride on water.

I saved the burning questions for the rental shop. This included whether there were any alligators in the lake following an earlier tragic death of a two-year old boy killed by one at a Disney resort. I asked my son if he knew anything about jet skiing, and he said no, returning his attention to his cell phone. Reflecting a "Just Do It" sports mantra, he had no concerns and his nonchalance added exasperation to my uneasiness. I explained that we could tip over and that he had to closely coordinate his every move with mine—no goofing around.

It was a gorgeous, clear, blue-skied morning with smatterings of puffy white clouds. We typically had a late start given my son's reversed sleep schedule, staying up late texting and Snapchatting with his friends to eke out his last pre-college days of summer. I squeezed in some cherished reading as well. When I looked at the clock, it read 4:44 am.

Really? The rental was only for one-half hour. I rationalized that if we made it there by three o'clock, we would avoid the "bewitching" four o'clock hour.

Upon our arrival at three o'clock, the man told us the jet skis needed refueling so we had to wait. Four o'clock was now fast approaching and there was no option for a later time since they closed at 5:30 p.m. My son headed to the pool unaware of my all my apprehensions. I scored a table nearby with an umbrella that shielded me from the hot sun, but seemingly not from fate. I walked over to the pier to get a closer look at the lake. It was calm with small ripples of beautiful deep blue water but I could sense the overwhelming mass of weight and depth lurking beneath it. The remaining minutes ticked away.

A little before four o'clock, my eyes locked in with the rental operator as he came for us. I didn't recall what I tried to say or ask—it was pointless. I went to get my son.

Life jackets on. Shoes off. Key in the ignition attached via a stretchy cord to be worn around the wrist. Facing the open vast water, there was no turning back. All my questions distilled down to one—how do I balance the jet ski? I was instructed to maintain my speed going through the turns and not to slow down which would result in tipping over. This was counter to my years of driving a car, but I managed to push through the turns, mentally and physically.

Strangely enough, after circling the lake a couple of times, my anxiety turned to restlessness having to go around in circles. And I had been so focused on the path ahead, I didn't notice whether my son was still on board with me. I couldn't feel his presence nor his hands on my life jacket so I yelled back, "Are you holding on?"

"Yes!" he replied. A second later, "Do you want me to let go?" he asked.

"NO!" I countered. I had pictured having a wonderful tête-á-tête with my son on this Kodak occasion. Having to shout over the loud motor quickly discounted this notion and the experience itself had to suffice.

I changed directions and attempted a few figure eights. I unwittingly topped 40 mph. I was relieved upon returning safely back to shore. We skimmed the surface of the lake never having to dig into its reaches.

The operator told me with a big smile, that I "did good"—that many men tipped over on the lake. When my son was asked how he liked it, he carefully responded that he wanted to do it with his friends the next time. His answer was fine with me. I did my part and that would be for the next chapter in his life. We had been out for thirty minutes and the clock's hands were almost to 4:45, give or take a minute or two. We survived with new journeys yet to begin. The universe had guided us through and all would be well.

Note to Self

Anne Haack Sullivan

Dear Twenty-Eight-Year-Old Me,

I know you don't want my advice, but now that I am older and, theoretically, wiser, I want to share some things I wish I'd known when I was you.

First of all, relax. Your "life plan" may seem off track, but trust me: Good things happen during life's little detours. I know that you're almost thirty. Friends are getting married left and right. The closest you've come to a date lately is that long-haired dude with a goatee you met skiing in California. Your grand schemes for baby-making and suburban living aren't panning out on schedule. But stop panicking and breathe. If things had turned out with the Irish-eyed architect you loved back in college you'd have missed great things. Like getting a masters degree. And all the perks of your "dream job" in advertising.

In a few weeks you'll be living in a new city. And yes! There you'll find that elusive husband you think you've been wanting. While you won't immediately know he's The One, you'll know you love his sense of humor when, instead of a stuffed Santa ornament or a glittery plastic globe, he presents the host of a Trim-a-Tree party with a set of twinkle lights adorned by twelve plastic fish. And, once you are married you'll pause fondly to remember the first time you met as you hang the "Mess-O-Trout" on the Christmas tree in your own future home.

I know it's been hard watching three best friends walk down the aisle in rapid succession, but cheer up. Instead of china patterns and life insurance you're focused on a fabulous new career in the pioneering field of interactive television! (Which will be a flop, by the way, but always sound cool on your resume.) You're not crying in your beer or spending more time with your cat. You're embarking on new adventures. Seizing opportunity. Starting fresh. And admit it: These last few single years haven't been completely hopeless. A job and colleagues you love. Standing inches away from Michael Jordan at a charity event. Commercial shoots in L.A., staying at the Four Seasons and spotting Oliver Stone at Spago. To many people, your life sounds pretty damn fabulous. Especially to the future you sitting in the carpool line wearing worn-out yoga pants.

I get it. You would have preferred to skip the last few years meeting men who consider Blackhawks jerseys "business casual." And to avoid the New Year's Eve date who chose a Jagermeister drinking contest over conversation. But it's funny. You'll miss those beer-swilling, shot-drinking hockey boys just a little when a pretentious ass completely ignores you over dinner in favor of an earnest, badly dressed think tank analyst who went to Harvard. Pedigrees are important in Washington, just so you know. So try not to be upset the first time someone calls Illinois a "flyover state." Instead, think how lucky you are to have friends from Portugal and France and Seattle and Miami who work at embassies and Georgetown and for Congress and the World Bank. Some will unfortunately like the

Redskins. Others will change the way you think about issues you never knew you cared about. If you watch the Sunday talk shows and have strong opinions you'll enjoy your time with most people. Except for that annoying Peace Corps alumna and her oft-repeated tale of bad drinking water and shitting behind a camel.

I know this part of your life has been a disappointment, but do not lament. As you sit in your bridesmaid dress, yearning to escape another chorus of "We Are Family," try to skip the self pity. Embrace the joy of making your own choices. The big ones, of course, but the small and medium-sized ones, too. Like where to go on vacation. How to furnish your apartment. What channel to watch. Which movie to see. Even buying brand-name garbage bags and pulp-free orange juice might be contentious once you say "I Do."

And that so-called life plan? Once you have a husband it is no longer yours alone. To succeed at this thing called marriage you have to work together. And your dreams will not always be the same. Like when he favors staying in Virginia and you want to move back to Chicago. Or he isn't keen on the blue stucco house you've fallen in love with. Or you find, despite a common goal of raising acceptable human beings, that your approach to parenting isn't necessarily the same. It's called compromise, but reaching it won't always be easy with a person who makes decisions using bullet points and spreadsheets while you need to talk things through over and over. It can be like that with husbands. Just so you know.

So please, Dear Me, take a break from that stupid roadmap while you're still in the driver's seat. Stop wasting time worrying about your ovaries. Or calculating how old you'll be when your imaginary offspring leave the nest. As you're nearing fifty you'll realize there are many things you simply can't plan no matter what your age. A child with unexpected challenges. Job crises. Major illness. Financial surprises. To face these, you'll need the strength to accept what life has given you. And you're learning to do that right now, as difficult as it may be. Embrace your life and all its unexpected turns. In the end, you'll still end up exactly where you need to be.

Sincerely,

Your Forty-Seven-Year-Old Self

A Particular Pair of Slippers

Catherine Davis

It was July. My husband and daughters were working at their jobs back home; my youngest was safely packed away at camp. I was going to spend a week all to myself in my summer cottage. Time spent alone in the usually bustling family cottage is a rare and beautiful thing, especially in mid-summer, and I wanted something special to commemorate the occasion. The wooden floors in an old summer cottage in Michigan are cold even in July, so I wanted a pair of slippers to pad around cozily during those evenings spent alone, supposedly writing my novel.

However, it being July, there were no slippers to be had anywhere, so I ordered a pair online from L.L. Bean for an incredibly extravagant fifty dollars. They would be delivered in about a week.

When the box finally arrived, it felt like Christmas Day. I ripped open the package and there they were—brown suede moccasins, fleece-lined. They fit perfectly.

What luxury! For a week, I had no one to answer to except myself. No dinners to be planned, no negotiations about what to do when. Almost every night I would build a fire in the old beachstone fireplace, tune in the classical music program on Interlochen Public Radio, don my luxurious slippers, and scribble away, pretending to be Ernest Hemingway.

August arrived along with the end of vacation. I left my slippers at the cottage. I don't know why. Slippers would come in handy during the depths of a dark and cold Chicago winter. Nonetheless I placed them lovingly in the bottom dresser drawer.

All that fall and winter I tried to order another pair, but something wasn't quite right. I couldn't seem to find the same pair I had ordered from L.L. Bean. The rest of the good ones were eighty dollars or more and, in my opinion, just too much money to pay for a lowly pair of

slippers. Finally, in January, I broke down and bought a cheap pair at TJ Maxx. They made my feet sweat.

I understand now that those Michigan slippers are sacred objects. They are only to be worn while in Michigan at the cottage, preferably when alone, pen in hand, listening to *Exploring Music* with Bill McGlaughlin on WIPR in the cool evenings. To wear them while walking around my regular house in my regular life would be a sacrilege.

Now it is the middle of March. Expensive slippers are on sale, but I don't care. I prefer to stay barefoot, dreaming of the day when I can tread the cold cottage floors again, wearing the particular pair of slippers I bought just for myself to celebrate being alone up at the cottage.

Driving

Judy SooHoo

Splendor. The window to my world is encased only by a membrane of the windshield of a car, the comforting seat snugly fitting me, its driver. From behind my uplifted face, I am drawn out to the wide expanse of my peripheral vision and beyond—to the pale blue and white swirls of the heavens. The opaque, milky sky, an ever-present backdrop wraps its all-encompassing arms around us with a loftiness belying its all-know-ingness. The sun is hidden but the powerful energy life source of its rays dance with the clouds. It pierces through the small cracks and crevices and is thirstily consumed by everything, animate and inanimate, reflecting back an unimaginable array of glimmering molecular forms.

Spires. Modern-day, man-made artifices stand clearly against each other like crowded pin-needles aspiring to reach higher and higher into a secret world. Trees with thin, craggily bare limbs stand stoically tall and soak up the reservoir of life to give back in the summer.

Satisfying. The vehicle responds with the slightest twitch of the tendons of my fingers. I am in control. Commanding or responding, I am in control. I have a destination and am headed towards it, but I am lost in the twilight moments of my world. No bothersome worries of my aging physicality or image. Sitting in my car, I am totally engrossed, body primed.

Sensing. I breathe its aura into my body all the way from my head to my toes. My brain cells explode like fireworks with familiar ever-growing, stronger electrical pulses of burning notes seared into my mind. My body obeys the tune—shoulders mesmerized by the rhythm and foot completes the beat.

Song. The Seventies' Aliotta Haynes Jeremiah's sparkling keys and rippin' strings playing on the radio. Windows down with air-soaked face and fully-steeped lungs surrounded by clear blue skies, deep blue waters, lush thirsty greenery.

And there ain't no road just like it
Anywhere I found
Running south on Lake Shore Drive heading into town

—Skip Haynes, "Lake Shore Drive"

Soaring. I am consumed, exhilarated and immersed. Alone in my car submerged in the precious frames of my being, life feels and is good.

Insomnia

Fumiko Tokunaga Jensen

Since early childhood, I have had difficulty falling asleep.

Living in a Japanese-style house, the ceiling boards were made of wood. Since they were waxed but not painted, you could see the natural grain of the wood. Awake in the middle of the night, looking up at the ceiling, the grain textures turned into monsters' heads.

Everybody was sleeping. Dead silence reigned over the house and I imagined that I was the sole human who was awake in the whole world. I was also worried when I had to go to the bathroom. In order to get there, you had to go down the dark staircase and walk through a long corridor. Some nights, I took my pillow and sneaked into my mother's bedroom.

"Mommy?"

She woke up immediately and lifted her blanket.

"Come in."

I slipped into her bed and the warmth of her body made me feel safe. I instantly fell asleep.

Early next morning, with my pillow under my arm, I tiptoed back to my bed, praying that my older sisters would not discover where I had slept the night. Unfortunately they always found out about it.

"Fumichyan [little Fumiko] slept with Mommy again! Fumiko is a baby, Fumiko is a baby, ha ha!" They would grin happily as if making fun of their little sister was the best thing in the world.

***

Throughout my life, I have had a sleep problem periodically. But recently I have had the worst case of insomnia. I managed a couple of months by occasionally using calming pills. However, afraid of making it a habit, I stopped taking the pills.

After several days without sleep, I became more and more exhausted and nervous. One bright Sunday morning in February, after almost a whole week of sleeplessness, I panicked. Since I was not able to get in touch with my doctor, I decided to go to the emergency room.

Fortunately there were only a few people in the waiting room. Before I was admitted inside, a nurse asked several questions. One of them was if I ever have had a suicidal wish. Afraid of not being taken seriously and being sent home without seeing a doctor, I greatly exaggerated the matter.

"Yes, sometimes I feel like I would rather die than not be able to sleep," I told her.

Finally, I was allowed to come inside to see a doctor.

"Please, doctor, my only wish is just one night of sleeping," I begged him tearfully.

"We called the commissioner—he is coming from Chicago. I can't give you a prescription before he checks on you, sweetheart," he said.

I didn't understand what he meant by that, but I started to realize that I had made a big mistake answering the nurse's question about the death wish. While I was lying on the bed wearing a hospital gown and had started to calm down from the hysteria, I regretted deeply about my blunder.

The curtain in my small room was open, so I could look at the whole space. The emergency room was not busy that morning. There were only a couple of patients with minor problems. Doctors and nurses were chatting casually. Some of them were looking at a computer screen. Looking around, I noticed that a young man with a guardsman's uniform was sitting a few feet from my room. He was pretending not to look at me directly, but I could see he was discreetly keeping an eye on me.

I felt guilty causing such a big trouble but at the same time, I secretly laughed to myself about the whole comic situation. Still unable to even have a nap and with nothing to read, I was bored. I got up from my bed and with bare feet took some steps toward the outside of my space. Alarmed, the guardsman stood up quickly and blocked my way out.

"Where are you going?" he yelled.

"May I go to the bathroom?" I asked.

He silently pointed to the corner of the big room, followed me closely to the bathroom, and waited outside.

Later, after a couple of hours, when I was thinking about the bright sunny Sunday outside and things I had to do at home instead of lying in the windowless, fluorescent-lighted hospital room, a short, round-faced man appeared. There was no hair on the top of his head but the lower part was filled with curly black hair. With a pair of black-rimmed round glasses, he looked amiable. With a kind smile, he said, "I am going to ask you a couple of routine questions. Do you feel like harming people occasionally?"

"Yes!" I said. "Sometimes I feel like beating up my husband when we have a fight."

His round eyes became bigger. "Oh! So you want to beat your husband occasionally?"

"Yes."

He speculated as to whether I was serious or joking for a moment. He jotted down something on his notepad and went on to the next question, "Do you have a weapon?"

I am a strong advocate of gun control. Columbine High School, Virginia Tech, and several other tragic incidents would never have happened if people had no access to weapons. I could be easily upset when talking about it.

"I am against weapons," I said flatly.

His eyes became rounder again. "Me too!" he said hurriedly, as if he was afraid of being scolded by me otherwise.

After a while, this kind man started to realize that I was not a suicidal, violent individual. He seemed to be relaxed now. He told me that he was an amateur pianist and that he had just bought the whole CD collection of Sibelius symphonies. I told him that my husband and I had played a recital at the Sibelius house outside of Helsinki. Then he asked what his next collection of CDs should be. I suggested all the Beethoven String Quartets. We ended up our conversation like a couple of friends. Finally, he said, "The doctor will give you a prescription for sleep medication. I have tried it and it worked. You can sleep tight tonight."

Looking like a kind, smiling full moon, he added, "Good luck."

***

I had a dream that night. I was at a gallery opening. A glass wall surrounded the gallery. Because of several big trees with green leaves outside, the wall obstructed the hustle and bustle of the city. Even though I knew it was in the middle of New York City, tranquility reigned in the room. My husband appeared with his typical boyish smile. He was wearing a sharply ironed white shirt, a pair of black pants, and a black apron. He was a waiter who was serving champagne and canapés to the guests. He looked like one of the hip waiters often seen on that kind of occasion. There was only me, except an elderly gentleman with a camel coat.

All the art works were about six or seven feet tall. There were jars, vases, Buddha-like sculptures. They looked like a kind of primitive art from remote tropical islands. Every single work of art had the same blue-green color you see in the Caribbean ocean. Several bamboo trees with the freshest green leaves were planted in between the sculptures. With the green leaves outside of the building, the atmosphere in the room was as if you were at the bottom of the sea.

When I woke up, I thought this could be the prelude to a deep sleep, like sinking to the bottom of a beautiful blue-green sea.

Healing Words

The Plum Pie Lady, Paula and Me

Ann Fiegen

Fork poised in hand, the Plum Pie Lady sits alone at the table, before her an untouched single slice of plum pie. The painting is magical, and for both of us it was love at first sight. "What do you think? Should I do it?" you asked. "Of course," I said without hesitation. "You need to have her."

And so it began, with you in that sparkly silver beaded jacket that matched your hair and me in my perfect black dress that took me everywhere, standing before a painting we both instantly loved. There was so much to love about that painting.

For me it was its serenity, the calmness of the woman's demeanor, the softness of tint in her face and hand, and the unique aloneness of that image of a lovely woman sitting by herself at a table. You were enchanted by the delicate posture of her exposed hand, the steadfastness of her gaze, the vulnerability of her expression, and the vibrantly red chair amid her otherwise neutral surroundings.

We took turns at that la-de-da silent auction at your fancy city club checking her bidding card to be sure no one else would snatch her away. Others loved the painting too, and so we returned often to ensure that no one outbid you, each time noticing something else that we loved about it . . . the delicate detail of the china, the hobnails that defined the shape of the lady's chair, the flowery print of her dress juxtaposed with the striped tablecloth and pointillist background, and always that elusive something in her eyes. At auction's end you owned her. You were ecstatic, and I shared your joy knowing that through your having her I would in a way have her too.

For years she hung in a place of honor on your dining room wall, silently presiding over your spectacular dinner parties, ladies' luncheons, and holiday celebrations. She watched while guests savored course after course of your culinary magic, a silent spectator as we feasted on rack of lamb, poached salmon, Christmas croque en bouche, and creme brulee, her gaze constant like our love for her and for one another. After a time she became one with all of us, yet another old friend joining in for precious times shared at your table, somehow remaining youthful as the rest of us aged slowly but surely through the years.

You and I got into the habit of addressing her as if she were real, a sort of third friend spending time with us from her place on the wall. "How's that pie, Miss? Go ahead, have a bite. It's not fattening, it's fruit." She remained silent throughout, her gaze fixed, her eyes holding a secret.

When you got sick it all changed. We three were still often together in your dining room, but no longer for celebrations. Instead we sat at your beautiful old mahogany table and mapped out the time ahead: you, the planner, intent on putting everything in order, and I, the nurturer, equally intent on helping you attain goals that often seemed to me impossible. As we sorted out books and papers, jewelry and linens, photographs and memorabilia, we recalled the shared experiences that were so deeply woven into the tapestry of our lives.

Our remember-whens spanned over forty years. "Remember when we and our kids got stuck in the snowdrift on the way to Florida, and I pushed us out in my tennis shoes while you drove? "Remember when we took that trip in the camper in 90 degrees with no air conditioning?" "Remember when you took me to the emergency room in the throes of a panic attack, and by the time the doctor came in you were lying on the bed with chest pains?" "Remember when we recouped from our respective surgeries at my house, watching mindless daytime TV and ordering take out?"

Over and over we revisited the myriad occasions when we were just two friends sharing experiences that spanned the course of our lives and now served to define the depth of our friendship. In truth, perhaps these precious times at your table were the greatest celebrations of them all.

The implicit rule was no tears allowed at your table, and I was the one to break it, melting down on a rainy September morning. "I'll only say this once, but I have to say it. My heart is broken, Paula."

"Mine too," you responded. "Mine too."

More time passed. You lost your glorious silver mane, and we spent an afternoon at the wig shop while you tried on wig after wig, seeking one that came even close to what had always been your crowning glory. "I can't do this," you said, and my "It's only hair" response belied a heart that ached for your loss.

I watched you get so small, childlike really, holding onto my hand when we walked, sinking into yourself as your illness consumed you. We once stood eye-to-eye, but now the top of your head was at my shoulder, and many times I leaned in to quietly inhale your familiar fragrance. I sometimes thought that if I could hold on to you long enough and hard enough I could keep you with me. If I never let you go, I wouldn't have to, and everything would be right again. But the truth was you were losing your fight. Prayers wouldn't be answered. The merciful gods were otherwise occupied. You were dying, and soon I would be left without my beautiful, smart, funny, generous, quirky lifelong friend who filled in all my empty spaces.

Your last gift to me was the Plum Pie Lady. "Will you take her?" you asked, and on the day that I did, I poured myself a glass of wine, and as Sinatra sang "In the Wee Small Hours" I pounded in a nail and hung her on my wall.

There are now no longer any secrets between the lady and me. I recognize what had for so long eluded me. As I sit alone at my table, I look at her and I can see the sadness. There is a sadness in her eyes.

Two Scarves

Judy SooHoo

The beautiful hand-made, free-form scarf in hues of red, orange, black, gray, shimmer and matte floats on my closet shelf. Intricately delicate and meticulously woven from fancied remnants, it belies its whimsy. Out of place, it sits amongst old, stand-by scarves, singleton gloves and weary, time-worn accessories from bone-chilling Chicago winters.

It was the spring of 2005 and the first time I had gone to the Harrison Street Arts and Crafts show in Oak Park. I was thoughtfully invited every year by my brother's significant other via her signature-designed post-cards. Gabriele is tall, lanky, soft-spoken and of German descent. Imagine my shock the first time we met in 1987, when my brother asked me to host them for a barbeque intending to tell us that she was pregnant. They both wanted the child but theirs turned out to be a stormy relationship. In future years, it was easier for my husband and me to maintain the peace by keeping our distance. We would see Gabriele and her son infrequently during family get-togethers that brought small gifts their way. When my son was four years old, I became a single parent and Gabriele reached out to me. She would call to advise me about parenting my young son while sharing stories of her son's teenage years.

Gabriele was pleasantly surprised to see me coming through the door of her small art studio that anchored one end of the annual fair. She introduced me to Pam, with whom she shared the storefront gallery. Gabriele's talents ranged from metallic sculptures and paper mobiles to charcoal and pen and ink drawings of orchids, her favorite flower. Pam specialized in multi-media compositions and wearable textiles.

We took a tour of the studio starting on the one side with Gabriele's works. Large-scale mobiles flying high above and flowers jumping off of easels filled the open space. Our tour to Pam's side focused on smaller handiworks of three-dimensional framed art and richly textured clothing and accessories. In a moment of girlish camaraderie and sisterhood that neither of us experienced growing up, Gabriele and I played dress-up with Pam's scarves and purses. Gabriele was an only child and I had just the one older brother. We cajoled, giggled and sought each other's approval while assessing our completed looks in a full length mirror. I selected a green, brown and yellow scarf that matched Gabriele in her groundedness while she picked out the oh-so-fitting red complement for me. Red in Chinese culture symbolized fortune and good luck. I wanted to buy the green scarf for Gabriele and was able to catch Pam's eye quickly and silently motioning my intent.

Gabriele and I went for a walk with her beautifully-maned collie, Conti, to explore the other artisans down the street. This allowed Pam to complete the undisclosed transaction. Gabriele recounted her visit earlier that year among her many frequent trips to her aging mother in Florida. She had experienced back pain during the drive down and talked about a prolonged congestion through the winter that we agreed needed looking into.

That afternoon I learned about her artistic side and was able to connect with her more personally—free of the usual controversial and strained family ties, relaxed and without pretense. Leisurely soaking in the warm sun, Mother Nature teased us with perfection that warm spring day and I was absorbed in Gabriele's world.

A few weeks later, Gabriele and her son came to my son's birthday party. While her son was ten years older than mine, the cousins enjoyed each other's company and got along lovingly. Gabriele left a present for my birthday which was the next day. I opened the box which revealed the red scarf and called Gabriele to thank her. Unable to keep such a long-held secret, I told her I had purchased the green scarf as a gift for her birthday which wasn't until January.

It became an early gift to her. She called me later that summer asking me for a favor. Very calmly, she told me she had stage IV lung cancer. The "ask" was for me to tell my brother. Gabriele, the health-conscious vege-tarian and non-smoker passed away six weeks later. My visits to her home during that time consisted of deliveries of Costco groceries and anything she had a taste for, as if buying in bulk interspersed with Trader Joe's soy bean ice cream would prolong her life. From her couch, I could see the green autumnal scarf draped over the shoulder of her headboard in the bedroom where she would give in privately to her exhaustion.

After she died, I weaved together the pieces of her life. She had a prac-tical side to her. In order to support her artistic endeavors, she became a dental assistant. She owned properties and was savvy in renovating them. She was in daily contact with her mother. Gabriele shined in each circle she chose and was judicious in others. She was loved by the children she tended to in the dentist office, admired in her single parent group and well-recognized and respected in the arts and patron communities. Gabriele relished the child she longed for and her gentle disposition was passed onto him. She showed incredible resolve in accepting her death sentence. Her insistence on accompanying me to the bottom of the stairs from her second-floor apartment during those last few weeks are some of my remaining memories of her. A more complete, mature form had emerged for me. It was one of wonder and awe of a multi-dimensional, intricate, free-form spirit—delicate and shimmering. Simply beautiful.

Flight of Angels

Marie Davidson

Sherry was possibly a celestial being who manifested when we needed her help and then disappeared into the ether. She did have a business card, which identified her as a hospice care nurse. I put that card somewhere but have never found it again.

My dad, Joe, was 93 and had been living at an assisted-living facility in Boston for two years. He'd made the transition to his new home, Springhouse, quite well. He had become a regular at the recreation activities and it seemed that everyone knew him. I knew he was admired and appreciated, as he had been for his entire life. When I visited him every couple of months, flying into Boston from Chicago, a swarm of the lady residents of Springhouse assailed me. "Are you Joe's daughter? He is such a gentleman." But with each visit, I could see that my father was losing another bit of his mind. It was a gentle sloping decline.

Joe had had a good life, remarkable for loyalty, love, and open-mindedness. His family came first, then his duties as a public librarian, Naval

Officer, and Red Sox fan. His greatest gift to me was his thinking I was just about perfect, despite all my imperfections.

One evening, Joe had a mild stroke during dinner, falling from his chair. He rallied, and then had another small stroke. My brother in Nashville said dad would make another comeback as he always seemed to, but I was not optimistic.

My dad's primary caretaker, Lynette, called me on a Friday morning, a few days after the second stroke. I recognized her sweet Dominican voice on the line. "Joe's going down. Come now."

I flew to Boston the next day and arrived at Springhouse at lunchtime. The facility had helped me arrange hospice care in his small apartment. My father had declared his strong wish to not have any heroic measures to prolong his life as well as his preference to not die in a hospital. No doctors, no IV, no tubes, no oxygen.

Joe was all smiles when he saw me walk into his room. The stroke had left him unable to speak but he was doing his best to communicate. Lynette needed me to get supplies from CVS, and I asked my dad if he needed anything special. He beamed at me and tried to form words. I got it right away. He was giving me his usual answer.

I said, "No, Dad, I'm afraid CVS does not carry a line of young wives." He nodded happily. I had understood his joke.

When I returned from the errand, my dad had slipped into a coma. His breathing seemed labored and irregular. I called the hospice agency and asked them to send a nurse. Thirty minutes later, Sherry swept into the room. She was a force of nature. She was tall and slender, with a nimbus of fluffy red hair, robed in a swirl of fabrics from neck to toe. A turquoise skirt with flounces, a rose-colored mohair tunic, and a diaphanous lavender shawl wrapped around her shoulders. She wore knee-length boots with metal studs and a profusion of bangle bracelets that made a soft tinkling sound. She also wore the most gigantic hoop earrings I'd ever seen.

Sherry took charge right away.

"Joe, how are you doing? I'm Sherry, your nurse today, and I'm here with Marie and Lynette. I'm going to make you more comfortable."

Sherry told us that my dad could hear us so we should keep talking to him, as we sat at his side. Death would come soon, in a matter of days or sooner.

She taught Lynette and me how to administer medications to my dad—a narcotic to keep him comfortable and Ativan to control the anxiety that often comes with approaching death. Her matter-of-fact compassion was exactly what we needed. As she was leaving, Sherry said, "Don't worry—if you follow these directions, you won't kill him with an overdose. I'm on all weekend and only a half hour away."

The next day, my dad had slipped further into the coma. Sherry had come back to check on him, still in her studded boots and colorful flowing clothing. She assured us Joe could still hear, and it was time to arrange for the last goodbyes. She instructed me to call his closest loved ones on my cell phone. She then talked to each one and told them what to say. "Tell him you love him, that you are going to be all right, and that it is OK for him to let go." I held my phone to my dad's ear so he could listen to his son, his brother, his son-in-law, and his grandchildren. With each call, I could see his body relax and sink further into the bed.

Out of the corner of my eye, I could see Sherry sitting on a chair, her eyes closed and her hands folded in her lap. Was she praying? Meditating? She seemed to be making a low, tuneful humming sound. Suddenly, Sherry stood up and asked if it would be ok if she took out her Angel Tuning Forks and summoned the Archangels to keep Joe company as he passed.

This couldn't be usual hospice care, could it? I didn't think my dad, a loyal Catholic, would object. I agreed.

Sherry lifted a small black case out of her backpack and opened it, revealing a dozen tuning forks, each nestled in a depression in the case. She said each fork was tuned to a frequency that would summon one of the Archangels. Sherry lifted them out with care and reverence.

"It's going to get very warm in the room once all the Archangels arrive," Sherry warned. I caught Lynette's eye. She looked alarmed. I was intrigued. We could use some reinforcements.

Sherry took off her boots, and used a boot heel to whack each fork. As a vibrating tone filled the room, Sherry called out the name of the Angel she was summoning—"Metatron, Raziel, Tzaphquiel, Tzadkiel, Kamael, Michael, Haniel, Raphael, Gabriel, Sandalphon, Shekinah."

"Shekinah?" I said. "Isn't that a name for the feminine aspect of God?"

Sherry did not miss a beat. Cheerily, she said, "And here's your new best girlfriend, Joe—Shekinah!" The ritual completed, Sherry slowly and carefully repacked the forks. My father's breathing had slowed down and evened out. Sherry slipped out the door and disappeared.

Lynette and I took off our sweaters. The room had suddenly become much warmer. We looked at each other with raised eyebrows.

At Lynette's urging, I went to the lounge to eat something. As I munched a tuna sandwich, I thought about my dad and his long and good life. I felt lucky that I'd had so many years of him.

My father stopped breathing about an hour later, Lynette and I each holding one of his hands. His breaths came widely spaced near the end, but each one was gentle and measured. I am sure he knew we were there until the end. I called my family. I called the funeral home. As Lynette and I watched over Joe's body I felt a rush of gratitude. For Lynette, who had summoned me to my father, and for Sherry, who had helped my father die with ease, helped us to let him go, and summoned a host of angels to keep him company on his journey.

Lynette and I reached for our sweaters. There was a sudden chill in the air.

The Art of Loss

Judy SooHoo

Loss puts you through emotional hell.
It can be the loss of something as
small as a favorite accessory or
something as big as a person.

We've all experienced the feeling of loss in the world of small things. For me, it was an umbrella that was imprinted with the logo of the school that my husband, son and I attended. Having left it behind at its first outing without seeing so much as one raindrop, its memory still triggers a pang of sweeping emotions. Even replaced, a fleeting image of that first virginal umbrella always surfaces from the part of my brain that should have disposed of it for far more important things but never did.

Small items can snowball becoming personified. When "lost" or stolen as in a robbery, feelings of personal violation emerge. Bigger things like job loss cut to the core of one's identity forcing reinvention and an evaluation of one's intrinsic value.

By the time we reach middle age, the loss of relationships scars our subconscious memory. Stinging betrayals that make life real for us defy our rite of passage into human kinship. Supposed undying friendships are tested until the deepest cuts irreparably sever our chosen bonds. Love runs astray and we veer apart. Relationship losses flood us with sadness, anger and feelings of being out of control. Eventually they wash away into painful lessons learned and déjà vu memories for the next time around.

I was only six years old when JFK died but a sobbing country told me something more than the assassination of a president had taken place. Over thirty years later across the ocean, Princess Diana's death was a second JFK moment as I watched frozen to the television set—another real-life fairy tale crushed. Whitney Houston. Robin Williams. The little three-year-old Syrian toddler whose body washed up upon the shore. Strangers can haunt us intimately with their everlasting power and lost potential.

The death of a loved one was the most profound and consuming of losses that took me to the edge of my emotional and psychological being. With the sudden passing of my husband of 18 years leaving me and our just turned four-year old son, I was thrown into a twilight zone.

Loss can attack anytime sending you careening through life.

When my husband died, my life's trajectory stopped short and its reversal began. When death presumed to come at the end of a long life comes earlier, everything afterwards is touched by its invisible hand. Actions are taken in preparation for one's own death—taking care of business, getting affairs in order, decluttering. Being mindful, seizing the day and living life to its fullest become code for how well one prepares for *it*.

At the age of 52, my husband's physical presence was *completely* erased. Untouched dinner, pictures half-hung, empty shoes, a surprise Father's Day gift to be opened—all frozen in the still shot of life. Only fading images, faint smells, echoes of laughter, voices and footsteps, vacant chairs—both favorite and head-of-table—and unfulfilled dreams remained.

During this hallucinatory cusp of my life, time played tricks with me. I continued in my old comfortable ways before jarring realizations required me to self-correct. There was now one less setting at the table, fewer dishes to be prepared, less laundry to do and cleaning to pick up, fewer clothes and things to buy. A household formed, but now with one less partner to help manage it, take out the garbage and clean up after dinner. Needs accustomed to and wants accommodated for, over many years, vanished just like that.

I would find myself looking for my husband turning the corner of a grocery store aisle, standing in a line of strangers or lying beside me. Driving along routes once traveled by him seemed surreal. Life as I knew it was repainted only in my mind where shadows jerked at heartstrings. There is a finality; there are no second chances, no extensions, only the litmus test of dead or alive with nothing in between—nothing but empty space.

My heart felt as if it was literally cut out leaving a gaping hole. Balanced between logic and fully-dispensed emotion, the two parts kept me functioning and sane. I tried to negotiate with the powers that be, proposing bringing my husband back to life. Eyes searched into the darkness that said I-won't-tell-if-you-don't-care, if my husband was returned from the dead. Pleas resounded in guilt that would have been more effective in trying to save his life beforehand, rather than afterwards, when it is too late.

I retreated to the now chilling refuge of my deafeningly silenced abode. All joy had been sucked away replaced by the thick cold gasp of lifelessness.

Self-confidence garnered along the way from youthful naivety or seasoned experience was gone. The inevitable second guessing tore me apart.

Loss pins you down twisting and turning to seek answers.

There is a plan (a reason) that this happened. God wanted him now. You'll get over it with time. I struggled with comments from well-meaning people trying to be helpful but left me resentful. And on the other hand, survivors of near death experiences had a purpose in life. Did that mean that my husband didn't or had served his?

I clung to passing truths from low hanging pearls of wisdom. "Only the good die young," and Tennyson's tribute, "Tis better to have loved and lost than never to have loved at all." Although I was able to continue with life without my husband, it made perfect sense that he would never be forgotten or "lost" to me, for this was once a soul with an essence. Losses of inanimate objects leave their ghostly impressions just like my umbrella. People losses are imprinted forever.

Loss takes away . . . so much more . . .

I was forced to face the loss of faith and belief in humanity and a greater being via all the unanswerable "Why" questions. Why him? Why me? Why this for our son? Why suffering? So richly debated, yet meaningless questions that spin unrequited into a black hole, and in finality, simply mandate acceptance, surrender and humility.

I was quickly stripped of my identity. We were a couple taking time even for weekly grocery trips. Separate lives that melded into a synergistic unit were no longer. I was thrown into a new classification—

widowhood: a single person but not one of youth and free spirit. And with that came potentially lethal personas, real and imagined: a party-pooper, an unpaired fifth-wheel, an odd-woman out, a home-wrecker. Loneliness and alone-ness. New paradigms unfathomable and old ones left behind inflicted further confusion to an already shocked reality, jettisoned into, unchosen and unprepared for.

Loss grows with you.

Losses—piercing, as with people, or inconvenient, as with things—are a fact of life that normally follow a progressive course. Left behind binkies and blankets give way to forgotten gloves, hats, umbrellas and keys, and graduate to the loss of relationships and people. This progression however, doesn't always follow a natural course of unfolding. It didn't for me. The loss of my husband was too early—in his life, our marriage, and especially for our four-year-old son.

As babies, when objects or people leave our sight, they seemingly no longer exist and we cry at their absence. We later understand that these objects and people exist beyond our view. From the law of physics we then learn that matter can take on different shapes and forms.

I relearned these lessons as our son learned them the hard way growing up. As a young child, he realized that Daddy would return after a long day at work. Coming through the garage door, he would be greeted by our usual game of hide and seek. Our son would wait ever so still and patiently jumping out at the very last moments to serve the ultimate surprise of glee and reunion.

I explained the loss of Daddy to our son by equating it to a broken toy that couldn't be fixed. Daddy's heart had "broken"—it didn't, couldn't work anymore. As horribly simplistic an explanation as it was, he seemed to understand because of his many disposed of toys. But the complexity of his feelings and the gravity of the loss revealed themselves. He responded when I told him Daddy was going to die, "But I miss Daddy!" to which all I could say was "I will too" as we held on to each other, tears co-mingling.

Later on, when our son would call out to me in his young, high-pitched voice that he lost something, a Pokémon or Yu-Gi-Oh card, I was careful in responding. I wanted to steer his pain away from the loss of some *thing*. I explained to him that it wasn't really gone. He just couldn't find it at the time. It had to be in the house *somewhere*.

Because of the loss of my husband,
I could face death and no longer feared it.
It couldn't hurt me anymore.

The confines of the walls of a house can hold our precious things and protect our children and ourselves for only so long. In the few short years that followed, more unexpected and tragic losses of dear, close family members continued to tear down these walls until they stood no more. The irony of which wasn't lost on me: weariness and numbness to death—and life—with deadlocked brain and checkmated emotions while on high alert to its ruthlessness and omnipotence in crushing the human spirit.

Our young son who needed attention occupied my daily void and was my saving grace. My sister-in-law was a welcoming shoulder. Along with a listening circle of a support group whose members shared the same fate—where inexplicable events and profound thoughts and feelings found safe haven—I was brought back to my life senses.

But the dull aching pain of death never goes away. In a cloud state or as a bystander in life, one never comprehends what has happened nor is truly whole again stunned at the injustice that has been dealt. Pain diffuses with time but raises its sharp claws during the highs as well as the lulls in life. The hole in the heart remains.

With age, I think of being an old maid, how my future would have been different, how my decisions have shaped my present. More clearly, I see what things I can and cannot control and what to make the best of.

Loss teaches us that people are not our possessions to lose.
They are a gift to us.
They belong to the largest of the world.

Although the family members who have passed are physically gone, each is nestled securely within our hearts and minds. Just as a liquid can take on different shapes and forms, they morph into memories—like being poured into a different glass from which we can drink and nourish our wounded, thirsty souls. Our experiences with our loved ones are what we are left with. Quality substitutes for quantity.

You can lose your way, but eventually, life teases you back in with the ultimate realization that we all suffer losses—that people losses and the accompanying pain are shared by all of us. Our pain is everyone's shared pain just as everyone's pain is ours.

My son is a teenager now. The other day I was looking for the newly purchased bag of throat lozenges which is a staple in our car during the cold, blistery Chicago winters. I turned to him and said I had lost the bag. He replied, "It's not lost. It's here somewhere."

On the Train to Auschwitz

Susan E. Cohen

Pies. I'm here to bake pies because the ones they serve in restaurants and the ones they sell in stores never have enough of the fruit in them. Which is why I like to bake pies, because I can slice up cartloads of apples and no one can stop me. I can pile apple slices all the way up the sides of the pan. I can almost layer a tower of apples and it's only gravity that can restrain me at the point when they just can't help starting to slide off the top.

They didn't serve pies at Auschwitz. Which is why I have fantasies about the place. I dream myself a pilot flying a huge plane aiming packages of ripe juicy apples on Auschwitz. When they landed, prisoners would rush to grab one and there would be enough so everyone could have seconds and even store some extras in their cold barren bunks. And then maybe the Nazis would have been inspired to start baking pies at Auschwitz instead of burning people in their ovens.

I'm at that stage of life now where, while I used to think that everyone else had figured life out, and I was the only one who did not know what she was doing here, I've come to realize that we are all hoboes on life's journey. That people suddenly find themselves riding on train routes for which they never bought tickets. I'm not especially talking about train rides to Auschwitz, but that image does occasionally cross my mind. I consider it a sort of new fangled self-help tool. No matter what predicament I find myself in, when I compare it to being on a train ride to Auschwitz, why it lifts my spirits immensely and certainly provides perspective on whatever petty grievance was formerly chafing at the walls of my brain.

Take a cancer diagnosis, for example—not so bad really, if you compare it to being on a train ride to Auschwitz. Everyone has probably at one point in their lives wondered how they would react if they were delivered a cancer diagnosis. I always pictured being ushered into a doctor's office by a very solemn nurse. And the doctor would shuffle some papers at his desk, then perhaps clear his throat and proceed in a practiced grave but sympathetic tone to deliver the fatal diagnosis. Actually, when a doctor did inform me that my biopsy was malignant, there was no office visit. He called my cell phone while I was pulling into a parking space at the train station and he got to the vital part of his message just as I was trying to artfully maneuver onto the train.

And it was delightful being on that train ride downtown to my Japanese literature class because I was not on the train to Auschwitz. I did not have to stand, I was not crammed into a sardine space with other desperate people, I was not starving and thirsty and dirty and having to urinate where there was no place provided to do that. I was on a modern train with a cell phone so I used that train ride to call an oncologist and an integrative cancer specialist and even a doctor of Chinese medicine. And when I had done what I could on the phone, I went back to reading "The Tale of Genji," which is a very famous novel, possibly the first novel in world literature and written by a woman at that.

You see getting cancer in America today (before the cancer has taken over your body) is really quite a civilized process. You get to wander the bland corridors of vast temples called hospitals, which are unnaturally clean except for the terrible flesh-eating bacteria that snarkily roam the halls sticking their contagious tongues out at our futile attempts to create a sterile environment. And there are priests everywhere wearing sacred white coat vestments while nonchalantly dangling a stethoscope from their necks. The stethoscope is some sort of primitive hangover from the time when doctors mainly examined you instead of the modern way, which is to order blood tests and then decide which giant steel monstrosity you are best suited to travel through.

And you always start out by removing all your clothes just like when you would arrive at the concentration camps. Only here they give you a steel locker to put your possessions in, whereas at Auschwitz they would take them away from you forever. They do issue you a number like at the camps but here it's on a plastic bracelet that won't come off no matter how much you try to stretch it. No, you need scissors to get it off and who remembers to bring scissors every time they have a medical appointment? Still it's much better than the camps where they branded you with the number, but it's the same idea---you have just become more of a number than a person. And you get issued these cotton gowns that are either pale green or blue in a tiny print that sort of looks like a rejected design for men's pajamas. They have yet to realize how appreciative women might be if sometimes the cotton gowns were lavender or fuchsia and patterned with flowers or generously sized apple pies and if they had a Velcro back that fastened nicely instead of the string ties which are too few and rather awkward to fasten.

But even the bland print gowns in those boring colors are a great improvement on Auschwitz where people either were freezing in rags or were pushed nude into the gas chambers. And here you get to wear a gown, which helps because you are usually laid out like a maiden about to be sacrificed on an ancient altar. They guide you onto a cold steel table that automatically glides into whatever machine they have determined might suit your condition. Then you pass through the center of these giant machines that blink or make unearthly clanging noises or zap you with unholy rays of radiation.

First though, an angel-type person that settled you in, runs for protection to her guarded fortress and then keeps asking you at set intervals—"Are you all right in there?" And of course, you say "yes" while part of your brain remarks "Would anyone in their right mind be all right in here?" But you are good and cooperative and ever so patient because you might have an IV in you at this point, as some contrast agent which is either nuclear or radioactive or some kind of toxic heavy metal is being injected through your system, so it's not the best time to protest or object.

Anyway, I've realized lately that most people are not exactly sure where their train is going or even which station they boarded on. No, most people are just riding, just trying to pass for normal, and almost everyone is trying to copy everyone else, while attempting to figure out why they are here. Of course, anyone on a train to Auschwitz would still trade places with you, even if you have cancer and even though they were not exactly sure where they were going.

Recently, I figured out that I've spent a great deal of my life operating as an emergency responder. There is so much opportunity to practice this unpaid profession with life being generously full of unpredictable features such as accidents and machines breaking down. It's what the Buddhists refer to as impermanence. It's helpful going through life to be a tad Buddhist, because it helps you appreciate the moment and keeps you ever so calm because you've been expecting things to fall apart from the very beginning so theoretically you don't have to get upset. There seems to be some unspoken law in the universe that any moment of peace is bound to be impermanent and that while passing through life we will inevitably be losing things, that anything that is impeccably clean is destined to become dirty, that all objects have a yearning to fall and break, although sometimes they just crack and you can get your husband to superglue them back together, but despite all the pretense you can muster, nothing is ever again quite the same.

No, life seems to be constantly attempting to teach us that our lives are out of our control no matter how skillful we are or how hard we try. And you can't forget that no matter how daunting or scary the roller coaster ride of your life is, it is so much better than the train ride to Auschwitz. If you get cancer in a civilized country today, you know that even if you are dying, they will try to keep you clean and warm and fed, even if it requires a lot of tubes and machinery and that they will keep trying to save you even when it is hopeless. Whereas, at Auschwitz even if you didn't have cancer, you were likely to be freezing, starving, improperly clothed and extremely overworked. Of course, you lose your hair in both these situations, cancer or the camps, but here they give you wigs and teach you fashionable ways to wear turbans or scarves while at the concentration camps, they used your hair to produce other salable goods.

As soon as I was gifted with a cancer diagnosis, I was enthusiastically informed by all official personnel that I had immediately attained the status of a "cancer survivor." This sounded too good to be true and as I reflected upon this bonus, I realized that you can't accurately achieve that title of "cancer survivor" until you have actually died of something else! Then I had a miraculous revelation—that in America today you might be inclined to consider yourself a cancer survivor if you survive the treatments. Imagine having a combination of poisons injected in your veins on a regular basis. Contemplate marching down a barren hallway to a steel door with a "Danger Radiation" sign on it like in a nightmare and being told to go in and lie down to get an intense dose of the very radiation you've spent your whole life avoiding. Which definitely does not suit you if you are the type of person like me who will request an invasive military-style pat down rather than go through the scanners at the airport. And then being informed that you need to come back almost every day for more-except on weekends. Funny how the optimal protocol for cancer radiation treatments coincides with the average business work week schedule. It all sounds a bit like a Nazi experiment, but, of course, it isn't. it's just the religion of modern medicine where we are all led to worship at the altar of science and taught to regard double blind placebo based studies as gospel.

When I first got diagnosed with cancer, I decided it would not be genuine to hide it. Once people know about your condition, they tend to be so solicitous as they inquire about whether any of your relatives had that cancer or whether you had all your checkups or whether you ate your vegetables because way down deep inside everyone's first reaction to cancer is THAT PERSON MUST BE IN ANOTHER CATEGORY THAN ME, for God's sake! However, the main problem with revealing your diagnosis is that forever after, unless you move far away, every time someone runs into you they ask if you are OK with a very concerned expression. And you may be OK for that particular moment, at least you hope you are OK, but you know that there are very possibly microscopic cancer cells doing fervent cartwheels all over your body and trying ever so hard to find a nice warm place to establish themselves and make a new home.

So according to the last test or scan you are OK, except they often miss things and for all you know the cancer cells are hiding out during the tests and multiplying a week later and chanting "Ha, ha, you can't catch me, I'm the gingerbread man." Which reminds me you don't want to be eating gingerbread if you have cancer, because those cells just imbibe sugar—they frolic in it and become fruitful and multiply so you would do well to follow a rather spartan diet, which is still a sumptuous banquet compared to what was parsimoniously dished out at Auschvitz. So now, when people ask me how I am, I like to respond, "Unbelievable!"—which they are not expecting, but which is rather truthful, being that for the moment I am walking around feeling quite normal just like they are, but at the same time acknowledging to myself that there could be some furtive metastatic cancer process going on about its' silent business.

As soon as people know you have cancer, they tend to remark that you look well which is a way to say what's wrong with you, you have cancer—you're not supposed to look well. And then you try to explain to them that cancer does not make you look bad—at least not until you are close to the end, and then you will not look bad, you will look terrible, because you are dying of it. No, it's the treatments that tend to make you look bad, like you are part of some ghastly experiment devised by descendants of Dr. Mengele. And you yourself have to come to terms with the fact that the train you are riding on is a cancer train, which you hope drops the cancer off at one of the early stations and leaves you free to ride on into the future, but which you also recognize might limit the number of stops on that line. You could, of course, freak out but that will do you no good, since we all know that stress is very bad for cancer, which is why cancer is extremely freeing.

Now that I actually have encountered cancer, I am making sure that I try to live every day as an adventure. I have started to pay much more attention to my heart and my guts rather than just my brain. That, just like a dog, I don't hold back showing people how deeply I care for them. That I do outrageous things and wear whatever I'm in the mood for and buy new glasses in a shocking color in case they're my last pair and say whatever I please as long as it does not hurt anyone else. And that I say "yes" to all offers of travel or new experiences, even if I'm scared. That I try, in fact, everything I wistfully wanted to do, but thought I didn't have time for, before I got cancer.

And to be an emergency responder, to be behind the scenes and to try and ease the path of all with whom I come in contact. At Auschwitz, it was easy to recognize that the tiniest gestures—the sharing of a crust of bread or the guard who chose to avert his eyes for a moment—made a huge difference. But even here and now, when you get down to it, every interaction with another human being matters. Each time someone we come into contact with gives us a sympathetic or encouraging look or word, it makes a difference. Each human being is trying their best to make sense of it all, and every encounter from the time we are little is a learning experience—a glimpse of recognition that this is what people are like, this is how I deserve to be treated, this is how people respond.

Because we are all on limited train rides. The compassionate force knew that if we were granted eternity, people would waste even more time than they do now—watching TV, comparison shopping, drinking alcoholic beverages, and gossiping about people who dare to not follow the rules, instead of seeking why we are really here, which granted is not easy to figure out, but it's not going to be discovered by just killing time. Most of the people on the way to the camps were not really sure where they were headed either. The conditions in the boxcars themselves were bad enough to scare them into the stark realization that their lives were no longer cherished by the people who now owned them. But even these trapped passengers could not foresee or imagine the terrors that lay ahead.

And yet there were very few suicides on those trains, because as long as someone was alive they could always cling to an outside hope. You might be one of the lucky few to escape, who manage to survive unbearable conditions and live to return to tell other people what matters. Even if you have cancer and it's not looking good and all the odds are against you, why there are always exceptions, there are miraculous survivors. I have been with the dying and very rarely do they want to give up. They want to still be reading the story, to know what the next chapter will bring, because that is part of what it is to be human, to have hope and to want to know how everything will turn out in the end.

I write this now not to scare you, but hopefully to awaken you, my fellow travelers. Whatever train you are on right now, try to appreciate every day that it is not headed to Auschwitz and you will find your life unbearably sweet. If you are on the wrong train, by all means get off—life is too short to suffer unnecessarily and you have the choice all of those other people didn't. You can disembark. So be a real hobo—wander and be on the lookout for a train that really down deep appeals to you. And when you jump on it, start baking the pies of your life. May they be juicy and infused with spices, abundant in apples and laden with love.

Acknowledgements

Thank you to Ellen Blum Barish, whose class brought us together and whose encouragement was invaluable.

To Susannah Davidson for making our cover concept a reality, helping us to believe this project could become an actual book.

To Kat Wertzler for transforming a hot mess of pages, fonts and formats into a beautiful interior.

To Deborah Cassell for her proofreading expertise and kind words about our work.

To the subjects of our essays—especially those closest to us—thank you for your inspiration.

About the Authors

Susan E. Cohen is a combination writer, poet, artist and perpetual student who remains passionate about studying religion and researching medicine. In her early 20's, she was doing research for her doctorate when she became seriously ill with a mysterious disease now known as ME/CFS. Her family consists of a fly-fishing husband, three adult children who collectively named her "The Dalai Mama," and Banjo the dog.

Marie Davidson is a writer, psychologist, and former librarian. She is a spiritual seeker who has a passion for listening to and telling stories. Marie lives in Glenview, Illinois with her husband and wishes she had a dog. She is fascinated by the workings of memory and, as a writer, takes to heart Ruth Benedict's observation that, "Experience, contrary to common belief, is mostly imagination."

With great trepidation, **Catherine Davis** prepared to enter the first writing class she had taken in thirty years. *I'm sure it's all octogenarians,* she texted to a friend. Little did she know she would meet a multi-aged, multi-talented group of women. Her favorite place to write is sitting on the porch at her cottage in Michigan, and she confesses to only a slight obsession with Emily Dickinson.

Trudi Goodman is a retired interior designer and active mother and grandmother. She has painted and drawn forever. Although writing came to her later in life, she views it as an extension of the creative process. The form is different but the struggle is the same.

Ann Fiegen is a happily retired mother and grandmother who writes a lot to make up for all that time spent doing less satisfying things. She also houses The Grant Street Writers' mascot, Winston, and a cat who is not nearly as charming.

Fumiko Tokunaga Jensen is a pianist from Japan. She is married to a Danish cellist. As a child she wanted to be a poet or a writer. She accomplishes both of her childhood dreams as she writes in her second language with a hint of the poetry of the East.

Susan Lyon has devoted her life to the arts and underserved communities both domestic and international. Her role as a family caretaker has afforded proximity to childhood haunts, inspiring reflection on her formative years. She has a fondness for Lake Michigan, old dogs and kids of all ages.

Judy SooHoo came upon writing to do something productive and creative in her later years apart from past lives that included corporate and family businesses. She is exploring her voice, her cultural identity and wonderful friendships. A Baby Boomer, she is also of the Sandwich Generation.

Ruth Sterlin is a psychotherapist and a grandmother of two. She has published a number of articles in professional journals but now wants to turn her attention to writing memoir and personal essays. Ruth believes, in the words of Anne Frank, "Paper is patient." And thankfully so.

At age 12, **Anne Haack Sullivan** aspired to be a Harlequin Romance novelist. Though the form has changed, her passion for writing remains nearly four decades later. When not writing, she may be found walking her Labradors, arguing with her teenagers, overcommitting to volunteer projects or binge-watching Netflix with her husband.

Made in the USA
Lexington, KY
17 September 2019